S104 Exploring science
Science: Level 1

The Open University

Life in the Universe

Prepared by Monica M. Grady

D1369016

This publication forms part of an Open University course S104 *Exploring science*. The complete list of texts which make up this course can be found on the back cover. Details of this and other Open University courses can be obtained from the Student Registration and Enquiry Service, The Open University, PO Box 197, Milton Keynes MK7 6BJ, United Kingdom: tel. +44 (0)845 300 60 90, email general-enquiries@open.ac.uk

Alternatively, you may visit the Open University website at http://www.open.ac.uk where you can learn more about the wide range of courses and packs offered at all levels by The Open University.

To purchase a selection of Open University course materials visit http://www.ouw.co.uk, or contact Open University Worldwide, Michael Young Building, Walton Hall, Milton Keynes MK7 6AA, United Kingdom for a brochure. tel. +44 (0)1908 858793; fax +44 (0)1908 858787; email ouw-customer-services@open.ac.uk

The Open University
Walton Hall, Milton Keynes
MK7 6AA

First published 2008

Copyright © 2008 The Open University

All rights reserved. No part of this publication may be reproduced, stored in a retrieval system, transmitted or utilised in any form or by any means, electronic, mechanical, photocopying, recording or otherwise, without written permission from the publisher or a licence from the Copyright Licensing Agency Ltd. Details of such licences (for reprographic reproduction) may be obtained from the Copyright Licensing Agency Ltd, Saffron House, 6–10 Kirby Street, London EC1N 8TS; website http://www.cla.co.uk/

Open University course materials may also be made available in electronic formats for use by students of the University. All rights, including copyright and related rights and database rights, in electronic course materials and their contents are owned by or licensed to The Open University, or otherwise used by The Open University as permitted by applicable law.

In using electronic course materials and their contents you agree that your use will be solely for the purposes of following an Open University course of study or otherwise as licensed by The Open University or its assigns.

Except as permitted above you undertake not to copy, store in any medium (including electronic storage or use in a website), distribute, transmit or retransmit, broadcast, modify or show in public such electronic materials in whole or in part without the prior written consent of The Open University or in accordance with the Copyright, Designs and Patents Act 1988.

Edited and designed by The Open University.

Typeset by SR Nova Pvt. Ltd, Bangalore, India.

Printed and bound in the United Kingdom by University Press, Cambridge.

ISBN 978 0 7492 2673 2

1.1

Contents

Chapter 1
Introduction

Up to this point in S104 you have been studying a wide range of scientific topics, including astronomy, biology, chemistry, Earth and environmental sciences and physics. In this, the final book of the course, you will use all that you have learned so far to investigate the origin of life. Some scientific questions are of immediate and widespread interest, and they stir our imaginations. Two of these are the focus of this book:

- How did life begin on Earth?
- Is there life elsewhere in the Universe?

These questions have probably been considered ever since humans looked up at the night sky, but it is only in the last few years that significant scientific progress has been made towards answering them, and only in recent decades have huge strides been made. The name given to the study of the origin, evolution and distribution of life in the Universe is **astrobiology**. The theme of life in the Universe will be used to conclude this course, showing how knowledge of the different subjects that you have studied and the skills that you have acquired are all necessary to help answer the questions above. The Open University is proud to be home to several teams of researchers who are actively engaged in the quest to understand life in the Universe.

This book is in three main parts. In Chapter 2 the origin and early evolution of life on Earth is explored. This is not only of interest in itself, but also guides the search for life beyond the Earth, because the better the understanding of how life got going here, and the more that is known about its basic requirements, the more effectively the search for life elsewhere can be targeted. In Chapter 3 the search turns to the rest of the Solar System, to see whether any of the other planets or their satellites have life on them today and, if not, whether they have supported life in the past. In Chapter 4 you will look beyond the Solar System, at the evidence for planets around other stars, and at how life may be discovered, should it exist, on these extrasolar planets. Chapter 4 also includes a short section on the search for extraterrestrial intelligence (SETI).

The use of websites is particularly appropriate in the fast-moving fields considered in this book. However, because specific addresses often go out of date, you will not find any web addresses printed in this book. Instead, you will be directed to the course website, where web links to pages with additional information of interest will be listed. Following up the web links is optional, and you should not spend too much of your study time pursuing these.

1.1 Getting the most out of scientific articles

On a number of occasions throughout this book you will be asked to read scientific articles, or extracts from articles. These have been drawn from a variety of sources, mainly from scientific journals, the popular scientific press and books. They were not written specifically for S104 and although we have taken care to select articles that, by and large, should be understandable by

S104 students, they have not been edited in any way, except that in some cases we are using an extract from a much longer article. So far you have had several opportunities within S104 to study scientific texts not written especially for you. Being able to extract knowledge and understanding from scientific texts is an important skill, and the following sections gives you some additional advice about how to do this.

1.2   Problems in reading scientific articles

You may find the articles you are asked to read, which are not written specifically for S104, will have one or more of the following problematical features:

- There is a lack of action required of the reader – no questions or activities – so it is easy to lapse into a passive manner of reading.

- Assumptions about previous knowledge are high, or low, or vary from one part of the text to another.

- There are gaps in the story or in the information given.

- Some parts are very dense, and subtle but important distinctions are glossed over.

- The links between text and figures or tables are weak, with perhaps no references in the text to the figures and tables.

This might all sound pretty desperate! It isn't necessarily that such articles are badly written; it's just that in many cases they were written with a specific purpose and audience in mind (reporting scientific results), rather than being a gradual, systematic development of detailed knowledge and understanding. After all, you probably wouldn't want to see questions in a novel (although sometimes maps and diagrams, and a list of characters with their relationships would be helpful). The best articles can convey the excitement of the subject, with an added 'buzz' and authority if the author is involved in frontier research. You can also get a general awareness of the topic and its context, and acquire knowledge and understanding too.

1.3   Some suggestions for reading articles

Here are some suggestions for how you might get the most out of an article. You have had opportunities to read articles earlier in the course, so these suggestions are really a reminder of the good practice that you should already have been following (not only in relation to articles, but to all course materials).

In this book, each reading of an article is followed by questions (or tasks) based on the article, and you should look at these *before* you read the article so that you can see more specifically what you are supposed to get out of your reading.

As with most scientific texts you will probably need to read each article more than once. On a first reading, aim to get a quick overview of the scope and style of the article. Don't get held up by any passages that you don't understand, and avoid the temptation to look up every unfamiliar word. On a second reading, highlight what you believe to be key words and phrases. You can now look up unfamiliar words if they seem to be important, but be aware that a general dictionary definition might not throw much light on the meaning of scientific terms. You can also use the course Glossary to remind yourself of the meaning of terms that have been introduced earlier in the course. If there is a difficult passage, you might find that reading the rest of the article brings enlightenment, or your notes on earlier and later passages might help, as might discussing the passage with someone (e.g. on your tutor group forum), or looking up some other text (including S104). Even if all this fails, do not despair, as in many cases this will not prevent you from getting most of what you need from the article for the purposes of this book. Finally, after you have finished an article, it is always worth trying to summarise its content in a few sentences.

1.4   Skills development

The scientific articles considered in this book clearly give you the opportunity to develop further the skill of active reading. You will also develop your writing skills by preparing short accounts and by planning and writing longer ones that:

- build an argument using information from several sources and with a specific audience in mind
- review the content or presentation of a piece of writing.

An issue that is of concern to writers (not just scientists, but novelists and factual writers as well) is that of plagiarism. This is when an author copies work from someone else, but claims it as their own. This work might not be just a section of text; it could be an idea or an invention. This is not to say that ideas cannot be used and built upon – that is perfectly acceptable, as long as acknowledgment to the original author(s) is given. This is why (as you will see in most of the articles included for you to read in this book) there are lists of references to previous work by other authors at the end of an article.

So when you are asked to write short pieces commenting on or describing work mentioned in an article, you are being asked to use your own words and, where appropriate, include references to other work.

It is appropriate here to recall from Book 1 Section 1.1 the idea of peer-review. This is where an article (or paper) is scrutinised by other experts to make sure that it is correct, before being published in a journal. There are many sources of information that are not peer-reviewed, and you must always be alert to the reliability and authority of the source. This is particularly true now with the rapid rise in the number of encyclopedia-like websites conveying information, often anonymously or with no references.

As well as further developing *skills*, this book also revises many scientific *concepts* from earlier books. Consequently, you will encounter a large number of technical terms that you have met before. Throughout the book, activities are presented that relate to specific scientific articles (or extracts from articles). In most cases, the articles are printed within the text but, for three activities, you will be asked to look up the article electronically through the Open University Library website. A list of the activities, and when they appear in your study sequence is given in the study calendar on the course website. This should help you plan when you require online access.

1.5   Referencing

You have met scientific articles in several places in the course so far (e.g. Book 1 Activity 8.2 and Book 5 Activity 17.1). Associated with these is a reference that allows you to pin-point the location of the specific article or paper in a library or electronic database. To do this, there are really just four pieces of information that you need to record: who, when, what and where. In other words, who wrote the article, when it was published, what the article was called, and where it was published. This is best illustrated with an example of a reference that might appear at the end of an article in the reference list:

> Hall, P.B. (2007) 'A Quasar with broad absorption in the Balmer lines', *The Astronomical Journal*, 133, 1271–1274.

In this example, the paper was written by P.B. Hall, it was published in 2007, had the title 'A Quasar with broad absorption in the Balmer lines' and the paper can be found in the journal called *The Astronomical Journal*, volume 133, pages 1271–1274.

This style of writing the reference is usually called the Harvard system of referencing. In fact, you will meet many variants of the style, perhaps with the date at the end of the reference, perhaps with the title of the article omitted, perhaps with journal name abbreviated and so on. Indeed, different journals often adopt their own 'house style'. The precise form is not really important; it is the information it conveys that is important.

If writing some text, and referring to the work contained in a paper such as the example above, you would tend to cite the author and year only. For example, you might write:

> Some quasars have broad absorptions in their Balmer lines (Hall, 2007).

Or, alternatively you might write:

> Hall (2007) identified a quasar that had broad absorptions in its Balmer lines.

If there is more than one author, then you simply mention the other names too. For example, Smith and Jones (2006), or Smith, Jones and Bloggs (2007). However, if the article has more than two or three authors, you tend to refer to (for example) Smith et al. (2007), where et al. means 'and others'.

Referencing material in books follows essentially the same format, although the publisher and place of publication (and sometimes the ISBN) will generally be included, and the reference may pin-point a particular page in the book (e.g. p. 23) or range of pages (e.g. pp. 23–29). So a typical reference to a book might look like:

> Stern, A. and Mitton, J. (1999) *Pluto and Charon*, Chichester, John Wiley & Sons, ISBN 0-471-35384-1, p. 44.

Note that some journals (including the prestigious journal *Nature*) save space by using superscripted numbers to refer to a reference list, given at the end of the article. For example, some text might read:

> A student may find spectral information about the bodies Pluto and Charon[1], and even find information about an usual quasar[2].

The reference list would then be:

> 1   Stern, A. and Mitton, J. (1999) *Pluto and Charon*, Chichester, John Wiley & Sons, ISBN 0-471-35384-1, p. 44.
>
> 2   Hall, P.B. (2007) 'A Quasar with broad absorption in the Balmer lines', *The Astronomical Journal*, 133, 1271–1274.

This style of referencing is acceptable, although most scientists feel the Harvard style is much more useful when reading a paper and trying to remember who did what, and when.

The style of referencing given so far relates to articles, papers and books. However, you might need to cite information from a website. This is required if the website is the *sole* source of the information, as opposed to the website being simply the route by which you happened to have accessed an article or a paper (in which case you would supply the full article or paper reference). If citing a website, you clearly need to give the web address (the URL), but because websites change with time it is crucial that you cite *when* you accessed the website. So a typical reference might be:

> Met Office (2007) Available from: http://www.metoffice.gov.uk/climate/uk (Accessed 16 December 2007).

During your study of this book, you will be asked to consider various scientific articles and papers. You will have a chance to plan and write an account that uses material from these articles, and so you will be able to practise referencing work in the manner described here.

Chapter 2
The origin of life on Earth

Earth is the only planet in the Solar System where life is known and abundant life at that. So it is a good idea to start your investigation of life in the Universe by considering the origin of life on Earth.

■ Recall from Book 2, Section 11.4 how the Solar System originated.

☐ The Solar System originated around 4600 Ma ago, from a disc of gas and dust.

When the Earth first formed, its surface must have been very hot – far too hot to support life. So how did life evolve from non-living matter? Before we can attempt to answer this question, we need to examine the origins of life and define what we mean by 'life'.

2.1 What are the origins of life?

The origin of life can be approached through four interlinked questions:

1 *When* did life first appear on Earth?

2 *What were conditions like* when life first appeared?

3 *How* did life appear?

4 *Where* did life first appear?

It is also useful to review what is meant by 'life' and the probable nature of the first life, as well as to consider the essential requirements for life, which you will do in Sections 2.1.1 and 2.1.2, respectively. Sections 2.2–2.5 then consider in turn each of questions 1 to 4.

2.1.1 First life: the universal ancestor

It is not easy to define life. Scientists (and philosophers and theologians) have struggled with a satisfactory meaning for years. Dictionary definitions include 'a state of being alive'; 'the sum of the activities of plants and animals'; 'the period between birth and death'. All of these are true, but none is particularly illuminating or useful in this context.

■ How were living organisms defined in Chapter 2 of Book 5?

☐ Living organisms were defined as those that had the attributes of reproduction, growth and metabolism.

The attributes of life discussed in Book 5 will be expanded slightly here to describe living organisms as those that have three interconnected systems: a system for the transmission of information (inheritance or heredity); a system for extraction and processing of energy (metabolism) and a system to isolate the entity from its surroundings and to contain its essential components (a membrane). Table 2.1 gives some characteristics of living organisms.

Table 2.1 Some characteristics of living organisms. Some are universal and others occur only in certain types of organism.

Example	Characteristic of living organisms
1	are composed of cells that carry out oxidative phosphorylation[*]
2	have a genetic code that can be replicated and that utilises four nucleotides
3	are composed of one or more cells that is each surrounded by a membrane
4	are composed of cells that can grow and reproduce
5	are composed of cells that have chloroplasts and carry out photosynthesis[†]
6	can transform and use an external source of energy
7	are composed of cells that contain mitochondria[‡]
8	are composed of cells that have a cell wall (external to the cell membrane)

[*] Oxidative phosphorylation is the sequence of reactions in cell respiration when oxygen is used and the 'energy currency' molecule, ATP, is produced (Book 5, Section 6.2.1).

[†] Chloroplasts (Book 5, Section 4.1) are structures (organelles) within plant cells and algae that contain the green pigment, chlorophyll; photosynthesis is the process in which chloroplasts trap light energy and use it to make sugars from carbon dioxide and water.

[‡] Mitochondria (Book 5, Section 4.1) are organelles within nearly all eukaryote cells where aerobic cell respiration occurs.

One of the points emphasised in Book 5, particularly in Chapter 4, was the remarkable uniformity that exists at the cellular level between organisms. This uniformity suggests strongly that all life that survives on Earth today evolved from a single ancestral stock – the **last universal common ancestor** (**LUCA**; although 'last' is often omitted). This is the 'root' of the 'tree of life', which shows the relationship between the three domains of organisms: Eukarya, Bacteria and Archaea. You will return to consideration of the LUCA in Section 2.2.2 and Activity 2.3.

■ From the list of characteristics in Table 2.1, choose four that are common to all living organisms and which must therefore have been present in the LUCA.

☐ The four characteristics are 2, 3, 4 and 6, so these must have been present in the LUCA.

None of the other characteristics is truly universal. In particular, (1) there are many bacteria that respire anaerobically and do not carry out oxidative phosphorylation; (5) only autotrophic eukaryotes (plants and algae) contain chloroplasts; (7) only eukaryotes (not prokaryotes) have mitochondria and (8) animal cells and certain bacteria do not have a cell wall external to the cell membrane.

Defining the nature of the LUCA can be taken further. For example, it is reasonable to assume that our earliest ancestors had the simplest possible type of cellular organisation.

■ Would this early life have been unicellular or multicellular, a prokaryote or a eukaryote?

☐ It would have been unicellular, because this is the simpler type, and a prokaryote.

Eukaryotic cells acquired organelles such as mitochondria and chloroplasts (the organelles in which photosynthesis takes place in plants) by taking on board prokaryotic partners (the endosymbiotic hypothesis; Book 5, Section 4.3) – so they must be regarded as more complex or advanced.

■ How does the endosymbiotic hypothesis explain the acquisition of mitochondria and chloroplasts in eukaryotic cells?

□ According to the endosymbiotic hypothesis, early (anaerobic) eukaryote cells engulfed aerobic bacteria, which subsequently became integrated into the 'host' cells to form mitochondria. Similarly, heterotrophic eukaryotic cells engulfed and integrated cyanobacteria, which evolved into chloroplasts.

What emerges from this discussion is that the nearest modern equivalents to the LUCA are unicellular prokaryotes. The first cells must have had a surrounding membrane that cut them off from the external medium and allowed some control over what went into and came out of the cell. They were able to transform and use energy to grow and reproduce – but the nature of the energy source is still uncertain. They encoded information that allowed them to make proteins by means of a universal genetic code contained in self-replicating nucleic acid (still used in all organisms). Whether the nucleic acid was ribonucleic acid (RNA) or deoxyribonucleic acid (DNA), however, is another open question.

2.1.2 Essential requirements for life

Perhaps the most important requirement of living organisms is for a liquid solvent in which molecules can dissolve. On Earth the only solvent for life is water, which is also involved in many chemical reactions essential to sustain life. So whenever and wherever life appeared on Earth, conditions of temperature and pressure had to be such that liquid water could exist. We cannot be certain that life elsewhere might not use other solvents – liquid ammonia for example – but the consensus is that this is unlikely. Water is probably the universal solvent for life.

Other requirements for life include appropriate sources of energy and supplies of the chemicals (atoms, molecules or ions) needed to construct living cells.

■ What two types of energy used by living organisms were described in earlier books?

□ Energy from light (used by cyanobacteria, algae and plants in photosynthesis) and chemical energy (e.g. that stored in food and released during respiration). (See Book 1, Section 7.3.1 and Book 5, Chapter 6.)

In other parts of the Universe, however, forms of life might have evolved that used different energy sources, for example other types of electromagnetic radiation.

There could be even more variation in the essential chemicals required for life. Only a small number of elements are used by organisms on Earth – between 16 and 20 (the number varies for different organisms) – and, of these, only nine are required in relatively large amounts for all species. The three elements that are required in the largest amounts (by number of atoms) are hydrogen, carbon and oxygen, in that order.

In carbohydrates the ratio of numbers of atoms is about 2 hydrogen : 1 carbon : 1 oxygen (e.g. glucose, $C_6H_{12}O_6$). In fats, there is little oxygen, and carbon and hydrogen occur in an atomic ratio of roughly 1 : 2. The core element, however, is carbon and cell chemistry is based largely on carbon compounds. Carbon is a remarkably versatile element and is by far the most likely basis for life outside Earth. But there has been serious discussion about the possibility of life based on silicon, and this cannot be ruled out. As silicon is in the same group as carbon in the Periodic Table (Book 4 Figure 5.3), silicon atoms, like carbon atoms, tend to form four covalent bonds. However, this alone does not suggest why silicon might be considered as a basis for life.

■   What properties of carbon allow it to form so many different compounds and therefore make it a good candidate for providing the basis of life?

☐   The ability to form long chains and rings of atoms.

Under the right conditions, silicon atoms will also form chains and rings of atoms, but not to the same extent as carbon atoms. Silicon forms a huge array of compounds when bonded to oxygen, and the Si—O bond is the basic structure of the minerals that form rocks (Book 4, Figure 4.11).

2.2   Timing: when did life appear?

If it is known *when* life first appeared on Earth, then this can be related to the environmental conditions at that time and hypotheses can be developed about *how* life might have appeared. To give you some appreciation of the timescales involved, Activity 2.1 constructs on Figure 2.1 a scale of the Earth's lifespan from its origin to the present day. Only two dates are labelled on Figure 2.1 – as you progress through this chapter, you will add others to the diagram.

Activity 2.1   Earth's timeline

We expect this activity will take you approximately 5 minutes.

Two dates have been indicated on Figure 2.1 at the moment: the present day and 4600 Ma for the origin of the Earth.

As you read the text, you will be directed to add further labels to mark additional significant dates; the figure can also be downloaded from the course website.

When you come to add dates to the timeline, use two colours or text styles (e.g. with or without an underline) to distinguish between two different types of date. Use one colour or style for dates which are fairly certain, and which may have been measured directly. Use the second colour or style for dates that have been inferred from other evidence, and which are less certain. Remember that you will need to add a key to the timeline, to explain what the different date styles indicate.

To start with, add a label at 2400 Ma to Figure 2.1. This was when oxygen began to accumulate in the Earth's atmosphere (Book 6, Section 3.1). Because this date is inferred from the absence of red soils in the geological record, the date should be marked in your second colour or style.

There is a completed version of Figure 2.1 in the comments to this activity at the end of this book. However, you should not look at this until you have completed all the parts of this activity, which run throughout this chapter.

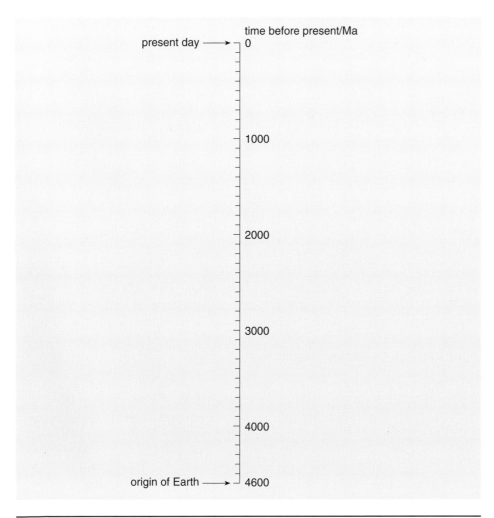

Figure 2.1 Timeline from the origin of the Earth (marked at 4600 million years ago) to the present day. The timeline is divided into thousands of millions of years, with sub-divisions every 100 million years.

2.2.1 Geological evidence for the earliest life on Earth

How, then, can the date when life first appeared on Earth be determined? What evidence should we look for that implies life is present? The most obvious traces of life are from fossils, the remains of plants and animals that have been preserved in rocks. But over the past 20 years or so, there has been a very fierce (and sometimes acrimonious) debate about how to identify fossils in very ancient rocks. Indeed, it has not always been clear which are the oldest rocks on Earth, never mind which ones contain the oldest fossils. The oldest rocks on Earth are currently thought to be the 4030 Ma Acasta gneiss formation in the Northwest Territories of Canada. These rocks are metamorphosed (heated and compressed) igneous rocks, and are therefore unlikely to contain any fossils. But, as you will find when you carry out Activity 2.2, ancient metamorphosed sedimentary rocks have been thought to contain evidence for early life.

In Section 2.1.2, it was mentioned that liquid water was the most important requirement for life. If life is to exist, then water must be present. Remember from Book 2, Section 11.4 that the Earth formed from a rotating disc of gas and dust some 4600 Ma ago. For the first period of its history, Earth's surface was kept molten by collisions from impacting debris. It was not until the bombardment died down that the surface cooled and solidified, allowing water to condense. When, then, given Earth's turbulent early history, did water first appear? There is a chain of reasoning that has to be followed in order to answer this question.

The presence of sedimentary rocks in the geological record is often an indication that water was present, either to erode older rocks, or to transport and deposit sediment. But sedimentary rocks are rare in the oldest part of the geological record. The oldest mineral grains that have been found are crystals of zircon (Book 6, Section 2.5), minerals produced in igneous rocks that are very resistant to breakdown by weathering processes. Ancient zircons were first found in the Jack Hills region of Western Australia. The Jack Hills rocks are a series of metamorphosed conglomerates, and are not the original rocks in which the zircons were produced. The zircons must have formed in igneous rocks that were broken down, and the resistant zircons transported and deposited in sediments that were subsequently metamorphosed. The age of the zircons has been measured using the U–Pb chronometer. (In Book 6, Section 2.5 you saw that the decay of radioactive isotopes can be used to measure the age of a mineral.) Most of the Jack Hills zircons have ages around 4100 Ma, but one or two of them are around 4360 Ma old.

■ If the zircons are 4100 to 4360 Ma old, what can they tell us about the Jack Hills rocks in which they are found?

☐ Because the zircons were formed in igneous rocks and were transported to the Jack Hills following breakdown of the original igneous rocks, the Jack Hills rocks must be younger than 4100 Ma. In fact, the metamorphosed sediments in which the zircons are now located are only about 3500 Ma old.

The oxygen isotopic composition of the main population of zircons has been interpreted as showing evidence of alteration by water, implying that water had condensed by around 4100 Ma ago, only about 400 Ma after the Earth first formed. At the time of writing (late 2007), this interpretation is actively being debated but, in the absence of other evidence, 4100 Ma will be taken as the date by which water was first present on Earth's surface.

Activity 2.1 (continued)   Earth's timeline

We expect this activity will take you approximately 5 minutes.

You can now add three more dates to the timeline in Figure 2.1: the age of the earliest minerals (4360 Ma old), the age of the oldest rocks (the Acasta gneiss, 4030 Ma), and the date when water was thought to be first present on the Earth (4100 Ma). The ages of the minerals and the rocks are more certain than the date for the first presence of water. This is because the ages of the minerals and rocks are measured directly, whilst the date for the first presence of water is an interpretation of the oxygen isotopic composition of ancient zircons, an interpretation that might change if other evidence comes to light. So, as discussed in the first part of this activity, mark the ages of the earliest minerals and oldest rocks in your first colour or style, and the date for the first presence of water in your second colour or style.

Knowing the age of the oldest rocks tells us when the Earth's surface solidified. Given that water is essential for life, knowing when water was present on the surface provides a starting point from which to search for traces of life. Unfortunately, however, the traces of the earliest living organisms are difficult to find and cannot be interpreted unambiguously. In the following activity, you will read a description of the arguments that have raged about results from some very ancient rocks (although slightly younger than the Acasta gneiss) that were thought to hold the chemical traces of living organisms.

Activity 2.2   Dating earliest life

We expect this activity will take you approximately 30 minutes.

In this activity you will read an article from a scientific journal. You will then extract specific information from the article that picks out some of the main points of a scientific argument between two groups of research scientists.

Article 1 'Dating earliest life' is by Stephen Moorbath, and was published as a *News and Views* piece in the journal *Nature* in 2005. A *News and Views* item is a fairly typical example of how a distinguished scientist is often asked to explain and comment on the work of other scientists in a way that can be understood by readers outside the specialist field. The author of this particular article is a senior Professor in the Earth Sciences department at Oxford University. He is a specialist in the dating of terrestrial rocks using radioactive isotope decay methods, and has a particular interest in igneous rocks.

The article describes a debate about the age of the earliest life on Earth. Moorbath is describing and commenting on work that has been published by one team (Lepland and co-workers). The work seems to contradict a previous claim by another team (Mojzsis and co-workers) that life was present on Earth as early as 3850 Ma ago. Both Lepland and Mojzsis have analysed rocks from Akilia in Greenland; one team found small amounts of carbon trapped within apatite grains, whilst the other team did not. Each group comes to a very different conclusion about the origin of the carbon, and it is this argument that Stephen Moorbath describes.

A few more details that will further clarify the article will be provided after you have read it. Most technical terms in the article are either defined there or have been defined in earlier books of this course and can be looked up in the course Glossary.

After reading the article, carry out the tasks below which give you practice at extracting information. Have a quick look at the tasks now so that you can make notes as you read.

Task 1

Describe, in a sentence, the geological evidence that was used to suggest that the Akilia rocks were 3850 Ma old.

Task 2

Give a brief account of the isotope data that was used to suggest that traces of early life occurred in the Akilia rocks, and describe the non-biological reaction that could cause the same isotope effects. (*About 70 words*)

You should now read Article 1, consider your responses to the two tasks and then compare your answers with those in the comments on this activity at the end of this book.

Article 1

news and views

Palaeobiology
··

Dating earliest life

Stephen Moorbath

··

Claims that 3.8-billion-year-old rocks from Greenland contain carbonaceous remnants of very early life have been the subject of argument for several years. The latest analyses look like settling matters.

How, where and when did life start? Geologists are helping to address these questions by diligently searching the oldest-known sedimentary rocks on Earth for traces of primitive life, either in the form of cellular microfossils, or as chemical and isotopic tracers characteristic of biological processes.

Since 1996, attention has focused on a small outcrop of supposedly sedimentary rocks, claimed to be more than 3.85 billion years old, on the tiny island of Akilia, just off the west coast of Greenland. These rocks have been too strongly recrystallized in subsequent geological eras by heat and pressure (metamorphism), penetration of deep crustal fluids (metasomatism) and tectonic deformation to preserve fossils. Hence, claims for life there had to be based on the carbon isotope composition of tiny inclusions of graphite (carbon) in grains of apatite (calcium phosphate). Writing in *Geology*, Lepland *et al.*[1] now report that they cannot substantiate claims for the presence of graphite in any of the crucial Akilia apatite grains.

The story began with the publication of two papers[2,3] claiming that ^{13}C isotope depletion (that is, low $^{13}C/^{12}C$ ratios) in Akilia graphite supported a biological origin. The host rocks were identified as a banded iron formation (BIF), a chemically precipitated marine sediment normally consisting of alternating bands of iron oxide (magnetite or haematite) and silica (quartz) that might, in principle, harbour remnants of early life. Such rocks are difficult to date directly, but an age of 3.85 billion years or more was claimed from uranium–lead dating of zircon (zirconium silicate) grains in a granitic vein cross-cutting — and therefore younger than — the rock that hosted the BIF. This date provided ammunition for the wide-spread popular claim that life on Earth began around 4 billion years ago. It also implied that earliest life coexisted with devastating global meteorite impacts, known as the Late Heavy Bombardment, which shaped the Moon's surface and, most likely, that of the Earth until about 3.85 billion years ago.

Following the appearance of the two papers[2,3], scientific debate commenced in earnest. I myself visited Akilia twice, in company with several participants in the unfolding controversy, but I could not understand why these banded rocks had been identified as BIF. Instead of iron oxide, the dark bands consisted of pyroxene (an alumino-silicate of calcium, magnesium and iron) and resembled igneous rocks from very close by. Genuine BIF occurs in quantity some 150 km to the northeast in the famous Isua region, where

the best-preserved 3.7–3.8-billion-year-old rocks on Earth occur. The Akilia rocks looked nothing like the Isua BIFs. Detailed chemical and mineralogical evidence soon convinced Fedo and Whitehouse[4] that the rocks were not sediments but strongly metamorphosed, metasomatized and deformed igneous rocks, and thus irrelevant for biology.

The zircon uranium–lead date of 3.85 billion years or older for the Akilia rocks was also questioned, because individual zircon grains are complex, possessing zones of quite different ages within a single grain that represents its long and complex crystallization history. The oldest zones indeed gave nearly 3.85 billion years, but this could be an 'inherited' age, older than the age of the host granitic vein, which some claimed to be no more than 3.65 billion years[5]. Other workers[6] then objected that the granitic vein was not cross-cutting at all, but structurally concordant with its adjacent rock. That meant that the measured age of the granitic vein was irrelevant to the crucial Akilia rock, because any previous field relationship between the two had been obliterated by tectonic forces.

Even more worrying was the proposal[7] that graphite inclusions in apatite grains resulted from thermal dissociation (at temperatures of about 450 °C) of iron-rich carbonates in the rock to iron oxide, carbon dioxide and elemental carbon, the latter with a $^{13}C/^{12}C$ ratio overlapping values indicative of a biogenic origin. This mechanism was suggested to counter claims for supposedly biogenic carbon in the genuine BIFs from Isua[8], which often contain iron-rich carbonate. In fact, only one locality now remains in the Isua region where association of graphite with sedimentary rocks leaves the possibility of a biogenic interpretation open[9]. Exchanges between 'pro-life' and 'anti-life' factions on Akilia have now been published for eight years. However, for many observers the ancient Akilia rocks have gradually appeared as less and less plausible domiciles for biogenic tracers.

Lepland *et al.*[1] investigated many thin sections of Akilia rocks containing apatite crystals by optical and scanning electron microscopy, combined with energy-dispersive spectrometry. This work failed to reveal any graphite inclusions in apatite crystals from the problematic banded rocks or surrounding rocks. Even the most widely discussed sample (known as G91-26), used in the original study[2], proved free of graphite.

This persuasive discovery seems an almost inevitable, yet highly problematic, consequence to the increasing scientific doubts about the

original claim. We may well ask what exactly was the material originally analysed and reported? What was the apatite grain with supposed graphite inclusions that figured on the covers of learned and popular journals soon after the discovery? These questions must surely be answered and, if necessary, lessons learned for the more effective checking and duplication of spectacular scientific claims from the outset.

To my regret, the ancient Greenland rocks have not yet produced any compelling evidence for the existence of life by 3.8 billion years ago. The reader is reminded that another debate on early life is currently in progress on 3.5-billion-year-old rocks in Western Australia, where chains of cell-like structures, long identified as genuine fossils[10], have recently been downgraded by some workers[11] to the status of artefacts produced by entirely non-biological processes. To have a chance of success, it seems that the search for remnants of earliest life must be carried out on sedimentary rocks that are as old, unmetamorphosed, unmetasomatized and undeformed as possible. That remains easier said than done. For the time being, the many claims for life in the first 2.0–2.5 billion years of Earth's history are once again being vigorously debated: true consensus for life's existence seems to be reached only with the bacterial fossils of the 1.9-billion-year-old Gunflint Formation of Ontario[12]. ■

Stephen Moorbath is in the Department of Earth Sciences, University of Oxford, Parks Road, Oxford OX1 3PR, UK.

e-mail: stephenm@earth.ox.ac.uk

1. Lepland, A., van Zuilen, M.A., Arrhenius, G., Whitehouse, M.J. & Fedo, C.M. *Geology* **33,** 77–79 (2005).
2. Mojzsis, S.J. *et al. Nature* **384,** 55–59 (1996).
3. Nutman, A.P., Mojzsis, S.J. & Friend, C.R.L. *Geochim. Cosmochim. Acta* **61,** 2475–2484 (1997).
4. Fedo, C.M. & Whitehouse, M.J. *Science* **296,** 1448–1452 (2002).
5. Whitehouse, M.J., Kamber, B.S. & Moorbath, S. *Chem. Geol.* **160,** 201–224 (1999).
6. Whitehouse, M.J. & Fedo, C.M. *Precambr. Res.* **126,** 259–271 (2003).
7. van Zuilen, M.A., Lepland, A. & Arrhenius, G. *Nature* **418,** 627–630 (2002).
8. van Zuilen, M.A. *et al. Precambr. Res.* **126,** 331–348 (2003).
9. Rosing, M.T. & Frei, R. *Earth Planet. Sci. Lett.* **217,** 237–244 (2004).
10. Schopf, J.W. *Science* **260,** 640–646 (1993).
11. Brasier, M.D. *et al. Nature* **416,** 76–81 (2002).
12. Knoll, A.H. *Life on a Young Planet* (Princeton Univ. Press, 2003).

©2005 **Nature Publishing Group**

Article 1 refers to a paper by Stephen Mojzsis et al. published in 1996. They did not report finding biological remnants (fossils) in the rocks that they studied, but they did find chemical tracers that, in their opinion, indicated that life had been present. They analysed apatite grains separated from a vein that cut across rocks within an ancient banded iron formation (BIF). They found that the apatite grains contained minute inclusions of graphite, and the graphite was depleted in ^{13}C. In order to understand the significance of this result, carbon isotopes in organic and inorganic sediments need to be considered.

In Book 6, Sections 2.1.2 and 3.1.1 you learnt about oxygen and carbon isotopic composition, and that differences in isotopic composition are reported in the delta (δ) notation. The differences are so small that they are reported in parts per thousand (per mil), with the symbol ‰. Carbon has two stable isotopes, ^{12}C and ^{13}C, and carbon isotopic composition is reported as δ^{13}C (said as 'delta thirteen C'). When carbon dioxide is fixed in photosynthesis, a lower proportion of the heavier ^{13}C isotope is incorporated into organic matter than the lighter ^{12}C isotope. So organic sediments derived from photosynthetic organisms are depleted in ^{13}C compared with inorganic carbonates. In 1988 the German scientist Manfred Schidlowski published data (Figure 2.2a) which summarised more than 10 000 measurements of carbon isotopic composition in marine organic sediments ranging in age from the present to 3500 Ma.

Notice that the δ^{13}C values for organic sediments in Figure 2.2a are negative, indicating a *depletion* of ^{13}C in the organic sediments compared with the inorganic carbonate sediments; the greater the depletion, the more negative the value. Because graphite in the grains from the Akilia rocks was depleted in ^{13}C, Mojzsis and his co-workers concluded that it must have come from organic sediments that had subsequently been metamorphosed (i.e. the organic carbon had been converted into graphite).

Mojzsis and co-workers interpreted their results as evidence for life on Earth before 3800 Ma ago; very ancient indeed. They came to this conclusion because of the ^{13}C-depleted nature of the graphite, inferring that it must have originally derived from organisms that fixed CO_2. Figure 2.2b shows that living autotrophs that fix CO_2 have similar δ^{13}C values to those of the graphite. This suggested to Mojzsis and his colleagues that since there was no known non-biological process that could produce such large negative δ^{13}C values, the carbon was a chemical tracer of early life.

However, as you discovered in Activity 2.2, Lepland et al. (2005) showed that there is a non-biological process that produces carbon depleted in ^{13}C. Rocks from the Akilia sequence contain iron-rich carbonate. When this is heated above 450 °C, it decomposes to CO_2, iron oxide and graphite, and the graphite is also depleted in ^{13}C. If this reaction was taking place as the original rocks were metamorphosed, then it weakens the case for a biological origin of the graphite. What makes the case for very early life even less persuasive, however, is that when the rocks were re-examined using instruments that could examine the apatite grains more closely, the grains were found not to contain any graphite at all.

Figure 2.2 (a) Variations in carbon isotopic composition ($\delta^{13}C$) in organic carbon sediments (lighter shading in pale green) and inorganic carbonate sediments (darker shading in blue) over 3800 Ma of the Earth's history. The height of the bands indicate the ranges of the measured values, and the line within the green band is the mean value. Most of the data are from the 1988 paper by Schidlowski. The paler-coloured box at the far left of the diagram are data for graphite from the Akilia rocks taken from the paper by Mojzsis et al. (1996). (b) Carbon isotopic composition of various types of living autotrophs that fix CO_2 and of recent marine organic and inorganic sediments.

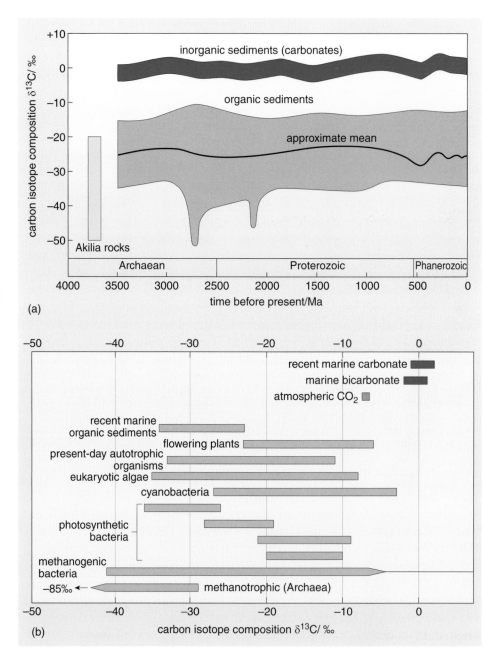

■ What inference can you draw from the discrepancy between the findings of the original scientists and those of the second team working on the same samples 10 years later?

☐ That advances in instruments and techniques can completely overturn apparently sound scientific conclusions, and so great care must be taken when analysing tiny amounts of material.

If carbon isotope data from rocks around 3800 Ma old is no longer evidence for the earliest appearance of life of Earth, what should we be looking for? Perhaps fossilised microorganisms rather than their chemical traces might be more diagnostic? Sadly, as you will see, identification of such fossils is as hotly debated as the carbon isotope data described above. For many years, since they were first described in 1983, the oldest microfossils on Earth were thought to be within the Apex Chert of Western Australia (with an age of around 3500 Ma; Figure 2.3).

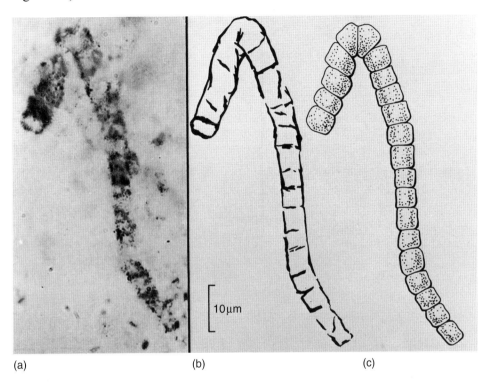

(a)   (b)   (c)

Figure 2.3   Segmented, filamentous carbonaceous structures found in the 3500 Ma Apex Chert from Western Australia. (a) Photomicrograph of the actual structure; (b) a line-drawing of the structure and (c) a reconstruction of what the bacterium might have looked like prior to fossilisation.

More recently, the origin of the structures in Figure 2.3 has become a subject for debate and, in the last paragraph of Article 1, Stephen Moorbath refers to the argument over their origin. These supposed microfossils were identified in 1983 on the basis of their shape – they seemed to be chains of crystals that were interpreted as ancient cyanobacteria. But when a different team examined the same material 20 years later, they realised that the features were more like sheets than filaments, and concluded that they had been formed by fluids percolating through the rocks, rather than by fossilised microorganisms. Indeed, the entire origin of the rocks themselves has been re-interpreted, from sedimentary (and so having the potential to bear fossils) to igneous (rocks that have solidified from the molten state, and so very unlikely to contain fossils).

The purpose of including the article on chemical and biological traces within ancient rocks is to illustrate how difficult it is to identify unambiguously the earliest life on Earth. This is an important lesson to learn if we are eventually to search for signs of life on other planets – and will be revisited in Section 3.2.2 where the possibility of microfossils in meteorites from Mars is considered.

Activity 2.1 (continued)   Earth's timeline

We expect this activity will take you approximately 5 minutes.

You can now add two more dates to the timeline in Figure 2.1: the ages of 3850 Ma (for possible chemical trace fossils in the Akilia rocks) and 3500 Ma (for biological tracers in the Apex Chert). Like the date for the first presence of water on Earth, the ages of the chemical and biological tracers are uncertain and subject to much argument, and so should be added in your second colour or text style.

There are, however, other features present in ancient rocks that can indicate the presence of biological matter. The first is the occurrence of stromatolites. These are finely layered rocks (Figure 2.4) produced in shallow marine environments by the trapping of sediments by colonies of cyanobacterial cells, forming microbial mats (Book 6 Section 3.1).

Figure 2.4   Modern stromatolites in Shark Bay, Western Australia. The flat, rounded mounds are up to about 1m across, and around 30 cm high.

The oldest stromatolites (around 3300 to 3400 Ma) have been found in at least two locations, one at Strelley Pool in Western Australia, and the other in South Africa (the Buck Reef Chert). Great care must be taken in interpreting features as stromatolites because, as for the features in the slightly older Apex Chert, there have been several instances where characteristics initially interpreted as being stromatolites were subsequently reinterpreted as being of non-biological origin.

In order to be convinced about the biological origin of a feature, it is clear that relying solely on shape is not enough. The geological environment must also be considered, i.e. were the rocks originally igneous or sedimentary? In the case of Strelley Pool and Buck Reef, the host rocks seem clearly to have been sedimentary, laid down in shallow seas, and thus appropriate for the formation of stromatolites. So it looks as if the first traces of life on Earth occurred at least around 3400 Ma ago.

This discussion can be taken a little further by considering the chemical as well as biological tracers. There is also evidence based on extraction of specific chemicals from rocks that life was present up to 3400 Ma ago. When cells decay and break down, they leave chemicals behind; different types of cells produce different compounds. Eukarya produce a class of compounds called steranes, whilst prokaryotes produce hopanes. Steranes have been found in rocks about 2700 Ma old, and hopanes in rocks with an age of around 3400 Ma.

■   By when had the first multicellular organisms appeared on Earth?

☐   Approximately 2700 Ma ago, because chemical traces from eukaryotes are found in rocks of this age.

As outlined in Book 6 Section 3.1, the oldest, undisputed biological fossils are those from the Gunflint Chert of Canada, with an age of 2100 Ma. So although this section began by finding that water, one of the essential requirements for life, may have been present 4100 Ma ago, it seems that a couple of thousand million years must have passed before life became established.

■   With all of geological time scaled to a hypothetical 24-hour day, how many hours elapsed between the formation of Earth and the time at which we are certain that prokaryote (or single-celled) life existed?

☐   The Earth is 4600 Ma old; the first evidence of life is at 3400 Ma, i.e. 1200 Ma later.

If 4600 Ma is 24 hours (or 24×60 minutes)

Then 1 Ma must be $\dfrac{24 \times 60}{4600}$ minutes

So 1200 Ma is $\dfrac{24 \times 60}{4600} \times 1200$ minutes

This is 6 hours and 16 minutes.

Therefore, after formation, nearly 6 hours and 16 minutes would have passed before conditions were such that life could leave the traces detected today. (Remember that life could have evolved further back in time than 3400 Ma.)

Activity 2.1 (continued)   Earth's timeline

We expect this activity will take you approximately 5 minutes.

You can now add a further two dates to the timeline in Figure 2.1: the presence of bacteria at 3400 Ma, as shown by the presence of both stromatolites and hopanes in rocks of this age and the presence of eukaryotes at 2700 Ma, when steranes are first found in rocks. The dates can be added in your colour or text style representing dates which are fairly certain, as the ages are determined directly by dating rocks. But remember that these are minimum ages – the organisms might have been present before these dates, but, as yet, there is no evidence for them.

2.2.2 Biological evidence for the earliest life on Earth

So much for the geological and chemical evidence for early life. If the geological record has, to some extent, failed us in terms of searching for evidence for the most ancient life on Earth, can the biological record be of any greater assistance? What can modern biology tell us about this subject? The technique of determining the sequence of DNA was described in Book 5 Section 13.4. Using sequence information from nucleic acids extracted from different organisms, the universal phylogenetic 'tree of life' can be constructed (Figure 2.5). This diagram will be revisited in Section 2.6 which considers where on Earth the most ancient microorganisms are found today.

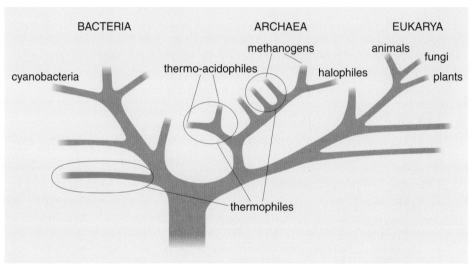

Figure 2.5   The universal phylogenetic tree showing the three domains (branches) of life; all branches shown have living representatives. Halophiles live in very salty environments such as the Dead Sea. Methanogens release methane. Thermo-acidophiles live in very hot and acid places. For clarity, some branches have been left unlabelled.

How does the phylogenetic tree in Figure 2.5 help to date the timing of the origin of life? The tree itself does not suggest any date for the origin of life. All it does is to indicate that three branches arose from a common ancestor early in the evolutionary process. Dated fossils show that photosynthetic cyanobacteria existed by 3400 Ma ago (Section 2.2.1), and so the time at which the Archaea, Eukarya, and Bacteria branched from a common ancestor must be earlier than 3400 Ma ago. In other words, life must have originated earlier than 3400 Ma ago.

Activity 2.3   A research proposal on the origin of life

We expect this activity will take you approximately 20 minutes.

Article 2 is an extract taken from a lecture given in 2002 by Professor Christian de Duve at a workshop organised by the International Society for the Study of the Origin of Life (ISSOL). It was published in 2003 in the journal *Origins of Life and Evolution of the Biosphere*. Professor de Duve was awarded the Nobel Prize for Physiology or Medicine in 1974 for his work on the structure of cells. He was born in 1917, and has officially retired from active research. However, latterly he has turned his attention to origin of life studies, and the lecture describes some experiments the author would have liked to carry out if he had started earlier in the origin-of-life field.

The selected extract describes two significant landmarks in the chain of processes that led to the origin of life on Earth. After reading the article, carry out the task below which gives you practice at extracting information. Have a quick look at the task now so that you can make notes as you read. (*Note*: the work by Stanley Miller mentioned in the extract will be described in Section 2.4.1.)

Task 1

Identify the two landmarks that de Duve identifies as helping to understand the origin of life.

You should now read Article 2, consider your response to the task and then compare your answer with that in the comments on this activity at the end of this book.

Article 2   Two landmarks in the origin of life

Christian de Duve

Elucidating the origin of life is tantamount to unravelling a long and complex historical pathway of which only the starting and end points can be defined with any degree of precision. These are, at the start, the organic products of *cosmic chemistry*, and, at the end, an organism known as the *last universal common ancestor*, or *LUCA*, from which all known living beings are descended.

There is now clear evidence that large quantities of organic molecules continually arise at many sites in outer space by mechanisms that are beginning to be understood, and, even, reproduced in the laboratory (see, for example: Bernstein *et al.*, 2002; Munoz Caro *et al.*, 2002). Remarkably, the substances thus produced include amino acids and other characteristic constituents of living organisms. This coincidence is too striking to be fortuitous; it suggests strongly that products of routine cosmic chemistry, brought to Earth by comets and other falling objects, provided the building blocks from which the first forms of life arose. These products could, of course, have been complemented by substances arising on Earth by reactions of the kind Stanley Miller and others have carried out.

Our second landmark, separated from these building blocks by a long, life-building process, is the LUCA, the ancestor of all known forms of life. The proofs of this single ancestry are overwhelming, written into the close chemical similarities existing among all living organisms so far investigated, be they prokaryotes, protists, plants, fungi, or animals, including humans. Particularly conclusive are the many sequence similarities that exist among genes that control the same functions in different organisms. Only common descent can account naturally for such similarities.

References:

Bernstein, M.P., Dworkin, J.P., Sandford, S.A., Cooper, G.W., and Allamandola, L.J., 2002, Racemic Amino Acids from the Ultraviolet Photolysis of Interstellar Ice Analogues, *Nature* 416, 401–403.

Munoz Caro, G.M., Meierhenrich, U.J., Schutte, W.A., Barbier, B., Arcones Segovia, A., Rosenbauer, H., Thiemann, W.H.-P., Brack, A. and Greenberg, J.M., 2002, Amino Acids from Ultraviolet Irradiation of Interstellar Ice Analogues, *Nature* 416, 403–406.

Much work has been done to sequence and compare not only RNA molecules but also DNA from different kinds of organisms. Complete genome sequences have been obtained for members of each of the three main branches, or domains, shown in Figure 2.5 (i.e. Bacteria, Archaea and Eukarya), which is one version of the universal phylogenetic tree. Remember that the branching is shown in the sequence of times at which it occurred, and that the more recently the branches diverged, the more closely related are the organisms.

■ Looking at Figure 2.5, what can you say about the relationship between the Archaea and the Eukarya, and Bacteria and the Eukarya?

□ The Archaea branch off the Eukarya in this figure, indicating that Archaea are more closely related to Eukarya than to Bacteria.

The tree of life shown in Figure 2.5 traces the evolution of organisms in a simple linear fashion, where increasing complexity is indicated by the length of the branches. It was assumed that the increase in complexity could only occur through gradual evolution with time. But more recently, the idea that the tree of life shows a simple evolutionary sequence has become complicated, with the realisation that genes can be transferred between species across the branches. This process allows evolution to leap forward by missing out some evolutionary stages. Even so, there is still a general increase in complexity of an organism the further along a branch it is situated. Notice also in Figure 2.5 that several of the branches near the common 'trunk' of the tree are circled to indicate that the organisms live at very high temperatures. These extreme **thermophiles** (from *thermos*, 'heat' and *phylos*, 'loving') typically live at temperatures of 80–100 °C or more in places such as hot springs around volcanoes and **hydrothermal vents**, the latter (also called 'black smokers') being sites on the deep ocean bed where very hot water gushes out (Book 2, Figure 7.4). Later (in Section 2.5.2) you will see that life might have originated in such very hot places, a hypothesis that matches nicely this finding that living organisms of the most ancient origin are thermophiles.

2.3   Earth's early environment

At the start of Section 2.1, it was decided to approach the origin of life through four interlinked questions, the second of which was to ask what were the conditions like on Earth when life first appeared. If one accepts the majority view that life had appeared on Earth by around 3400 Ma ago, then, in order to develop hypotheses about how this might have happened, you need to know what conditions were like then and earlier. What was the temperature and the composition of the atmosphere and of the oceans?

The Earth itself provides virtually no clues because no rocks and very little evidence of other kinds remain from before about 4000 Ma ago. Instead, we must turn to astrophysicists and planetary scientists for information about the Moon and other planets, and for information about other stars to compare with our Sun. Based on such information, Sections 2.3.1–2.3.3 describe factors that are generally believed to have had major influences on the Earth's early environment.

2.3.1   Bombardment from space

The first 1000 Ma of Earth's history is known as the Hadean Era (from the Greek *Hades*, meaning hell). It is very likely that throughout this time Earth was indeed a hellish place. About 40–50 Ma years after the Sun formed, the Earth was hit by an impactor about the size of Mars. The result of this collision was that an enormous amount of material was removed from the Earth, which eventually came together (along with material from the impactor) to form the Moon. Some material from the impactor also got added to Earth. From the Moon's formation until about 3800 Ma ago, the Earth was subjected to continued heavy bombardment by bodies from space left over from the formation of planets, such as:

- comets, which are composed of ice mixed with rocky dust and organic compounds, and typically are up to a few kilometres across

- rocky bodies, which have a continuous size distribution ranging from a few the size of our Moon, to larger numbers of asteroids (hundreds of metres to hundreds of kilometres across), to even larger numbers of bodies up to several metres in size called meteoroids (or meteorites if they survive to reach the Earth's surface), to huge numbers of tiny dust particles.

Bombardment of the Earth by comets and asteroids had the potential to influence the origin of life in two ways. These impacting bodies delivered water and organic compounds to Earth, and so could provide the ingredients for life to get going. The effects of impact also have the potential to wipe out any life that has struggled to evolve. Other planetary bodies are also affected in the same way.

2.3.2 Carbon in meteorites

Meteorites are fragments of asteroids that have landed on Earth. One group of meteorites is particularly important for discussions about delivery of the building blocks of life to Earth (Figure 2.6). The group is that of the **carbonaceous chondrites**, most particularly the subgroups CI and CM (the meaning of these abbreviations is not relevant here). These are meteorites that are chemically very 'primitive' and, as their name suggests, they contain carbon. Carbonaceous chondrites are comparatively rare in meteorite collections, but it is thought that they have remained unaltered from their time of formation 4600 Ma ago (hence 'primitive').

1.5 cm

Figure 2.6 A fist-sized piece of the Murchison meteorite, a carbonaceous chondrite which fell in Victoria, Australia in February 1969. It is a dark, fine-grained rock that contains around 2% by mass of organic carbon, including amino and carboxylic acids.

The CI and CM chondrites are made of rocky minerals mixed with around 2–4% by mass carbon present as organic compounds. Some of the organic molecules are soluble, but most of the organic material occurs as an acid-insoluble phase. This is a jumbled mixture of organic compounds that is inert to acid attack (hence 'acid-insoluble'); indeed, this is a property that is exploited in the laboratory when meteorites, or terrestrial rocks, are treated with acids to dissolve silicates, carbonates, sulfates, etc., leaving behind a residue of inert carbonaceous material.

On Earth acid-insoluble carbon is found in sediments. Coal is an example of a carbonaceous material that is acid-insoluble; crude oil, which is produced by the action of sediment burial and subsequent heating, is another example. In both cases, oil and coal are altered products of decayed biological materials (easily assessed using techniques of microscopy or other analytical methods). But acid-insoluble carbon is not necessarily formed by biological processes. Polycyclic aromatic hydrocarbons (Activity 3.3), as the name may imply, are complex compounds consisting of carbon and hydrogen only, that contain several benzene rings (Book 4 Section 12.2.4) fused together. They can be produced by non-biological processes; when concentrated and heated they transform into acid-insoluble components. It is a non-biological (or abiogenic) origin that most satisfactorily describes the acid-insoluble organic compounds in carbonaceous chondrites. The soluble organic compounds are relatively simple molecules and are also non-biological in origin and, though biological 'signatures' are sometimes seen, these are always artefacts resulting from contamination by terrestrial compounds.

■   What makes carbonaceous chondrites so important as far as extraterrestrial life is concerned?

☐   Carbonaceous chondrites contain significant amounts of organic compounds that could have acted as the building blocks of life. Because other planetary bodies in the Solar System as well as the Earth were bombarded by asteroids (including the parent objects of carbonaceous chondrites) and comets, the building blocks of life must have been delivered throughout the Solar System.

Murchison (Figure 2.6) is one CM meteorite that contains biologically important compounds. As well as water (about 12% by mass) and amino acids (10–20 ppm), there are the complex organic bases found in DNA and RNA (Book 5 Section 10.1): single-ringed (about 1 ppm), and two-ringed (about 0.05 ppm). But even though the overall carbon content of Murchison is 2.0–2.5% by mass (i.e. 20 000–25 000 ppm) these biologically important molecules only constitute overall about 20 ppm of the carbon, i.e. only about 0.1% of the total mass of carbon.

Question 2.1

Between 4600 and 4000 Ma ago, the surface of the primitive Earth was bombarded by materials which probably had an overall composition not very different from that of the Murchison meteorite. What kinds of biologically significant materials would have been deposited on to the primitive Earth at this time?

So impactors from space have the potential to deliver the building blocks of life to Earth. This is not to suggest that they actually delivered life. That (controversial) possibility is discussed in Section 2.5.3.

Much of the evidence for a heavy bombardment comes from observations of impact craters on the Moon and on certain other planets in the Solar System. The point here is that the early Earth would have been a very unstable place, particularly before about 4100 Ma ago, with large impacts generating a great deal of heat (enough to boil off whole oceans according to some scientists) and throwing up huge clouds of dust and steam. It is difficult to see how life could have originated in such conditions. Furthermore, evidence from lunar craters suggests that, although the heavy bombardment gradually declined, there might have been an increase towards its end – a **late heavy bombardment** – ending about 3800 Ma ago.

■   How does this information match the evidence in Section 2.2 about the timing of the origin of life on Earth?

☐   The suggestion in Section 2.2 was that life was present at least 3400 Ma ago. This is after the end of the late heavy bombardment. Although life might have originated before 3400 Ma ago, we have no evidence for that preserved in rocks or minerals.

Activity 2.1 (continued) Earth's timeline

We expect this activity will take you approximately 5 minutes.

You can now add another date to the timeline in Figure 2.1: the date of the late heavy bombardment (3800 Ma). The date should be added in your colour or text style representing data which are relatively uncertain, as it is inferred from observation of craters on the Moon, and not from the absolute measurement of a rock.

You have now completed this activity, so you should look at the comments at the end of this book.

Even without a late surge, the bombardment 4000 Ma ago would still have been heavy. It is possible that there were earlier forms of life that originated prior to the bombardment, but which were wiped out. This process might have occurred more than once. Indeed, there could have been several origins and extinctions. Living organisms might even have arrived with the late heavy bombardment – a very contentious idea explored in Section 2.5.3.

2.3.3 The early atmosphere and oceans

When did Earth's atmosphere form, and how has it changed with time? In Sections 2.3.1 and 2.3.2, bombardment of the Earth by impactors was discussed. How did this affect the atmosphere? You will now consider this aspect of Earth's evolutionary history by completing Activity 2.4.

Activity 2.4 Earth's earliest atmosphere

We expect this activity will take you approximately 20 minutes.

Article 3 is an extract from a paper entitled 'The Earth's earliest atmosphere' by Kevin Zahnle, and discusses how the atmosphere formed and changed in composition over the first 1000 Ma of Earth's history. The paper appeared in a magazine, *Elements*, which is published jointly by several professional societies (see the link on the course website). Every two months, the magazine takes a specific theme, and commissions leading scientists to write a series of reviews on that theme. The reviews are kept at a fairly general level so that they can be understood by non-specialists. The issue from which this extract was taken had five papers discussing 'The Early Earth', and you might find all of the papers interesting and of relevance to other sections of this book. Here, however, the focus is on the early atmosphere.

Kevin Zahnle is a staff scientist at NASA's Ames Research Center in California. He specialises in the study of the atmospheres of the rocky planets, and how they have changed with time, particularly through bombardment by asteroids and comets.

The extract taken from Zahnle's paper is from a section called 'After the Moon-forming impact'. It is illustrated with a figure (Figure 3 in the article) which is redrawn here in a slightly simplified form as Figure 2.7. Refer to this figure rather than the one in the article, when you are carrying out the tasks below. Notice again that the article contains references to work by other scientists.

In the first part of the extract, Zahnle considers the composition of the atmosphere immediately following formation of the Moon. In the final part of the extract, he looks at how the presence of an ocean of liquid water would influence the atmosphere. The details of this are not important for the purposes of this book, but are interesting given current concerns about global warming and the greenhouse effect.

The period of time that the author covers takes us up to about 3600 Ma ago, just before we have evidence for life on Earth. The period known as the late heavy bombardment is one of the final events of the Hadean era.

After reading the article, carry out the tasks below which give you practice at extracting information. Have a quick look at the tasks now so that you can make notes as you read.

Task 1

Describe the probable composition of the Earth's earliest atmosphere after the Moon formed.

Task 2

Use Figure 2.7 to describe how the temperature of the Earth's surface changed through the Hadean era.

You should now read Article 3, consider your responses to the two tasks and then compare your answers with those in the comments on this activity at the end of this book.

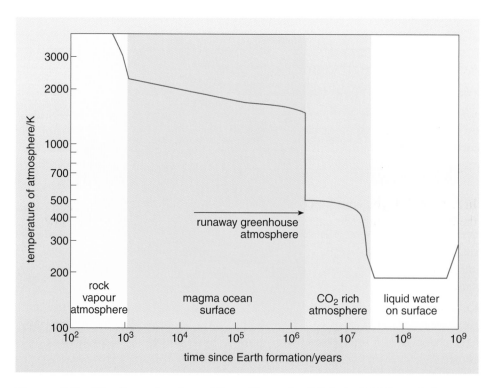

Figure 2.7   The figure is adapted from Figure 3 of Zahnle (2006), and shows how the Earth's surface temperature was thought to vary during the Hadean, from just after the Moon-forming impact up until the Late Heavy Bombardment. Note that both axes are logarithmic scales.

Article 3   After the Moon-forming impact

Kevin J. Zahnle

Although the Moon-forming impact may not have been the last big impact, it probably was the last time that Earth was hit by another planet. The impact is currently thought to have occurred at around 40–50 Ma (see Halliday 2006). By coincidence the Sun reached the Main Sequence at ~50Ma. This is a good place to take up Earth's story (FIG. 3).

Most of the mantle was melted by the Moon-forming impact, and some of it was vaporized (Canup 2004). Immediately after the impact, the atmosphere was mostly rock vapour topped by ~2500K silicate clouds. For a thousand years the silicate clouds defined the visible face of the planet. The new Earth might have looked something like a small star or a fiery Jupiter wrapped in incandescent clouds. Silicates condensed and rained out at a rate of about a meter a day. Mixed into the atmosphere, at first as relatively minor constituents but becoming increasingly prominent as the silicates fell out, were the volatiles. Because convective cooling requires that every parcel be brought to the cloud tops to cool, the mantle should have largely degassed, with the notable exception of water, which remained mostly in the molten mantle and which degassed as the mantle froze. When the silicates were gone, a hot CO_2–CO–H_2O–H_2 atmosphere remained, although at first most of Earth's water would have been dissolved in the molten mantle. Also left in the atmosphere were nitrogen, the noble gases, and possibly moderately volatile elements such as Zn and Pb, some of which did not fully condense until after the surface of the magma ocean froze.

How thick the atmosphere was is debatable. The Moon-forming impact may or may not have expelled a significant fraction of Earth's pre-existing volatiles, and Earth may or may not have had abundant volatiles to lose. A primary H_2 atmosphere, because of its low mean molecular weight would have readily escaped. But a secondary atmosphere would have to be pushed off. It is generally agreed that the volatiles on the side of Earth that got hit were lost, but it is an open question how volatiles on the other side could be lost. Recent theory suggests that the answer depends on whether there had been a deep liquid-water ocean on the surface. A thin atmosphere above a thick water ocean can be expelled. Otherwise the atmosphere is retained (Genda and Abe 2005). One notes that water is retained in either event. The view taken here is that the planet that became Earth was water rich.

References:

Canup, R.M. (2004) 'Simulations of a late lunar-forming impact', *Icarus*, 168, 433–56.

Genda, H. and Abe, Y. (2005) 'Enhanced atmospheric loss on protoplanets at the giant impact phase in the presence of oceans', *Nature*, 433, 842–4.

Halliday, A.N. (2006) 'The origin of the Earth – What's New?', *Elements*, 2, 205–10.

In Activity 2.4, you considered what had happened to the atmosphere up to the late heavy bombardment. An additional source of gases, especially water vapour, came from the comets and asteroids that impacted the Earth during the heavy bombardment. What happened after the late heavy bombardment when the Earth's surface and atmosphere stabilised? Based on comparisons with neighbouring planets Mars and Venus, it seems most likely that the atmosphere formed partly through the release of gases trapped within the Earth. Volcanoes belched out gases, including water vapour, which were retained as an atmosphere by the gravitational attraction of the Earth. Such outgassing of a similar mixture of gases still goes on today.

■ As well as water vapour, what gas(es) would you expect to have been present in substantial quantities in Earth's early atmosphere following the late heavy bombardment? Which gas (that is abundant today) would have been present in very low concentrations?

☐ Other gases present in substantial quantities are carbon dioxide (CO_2) and nitrogen (N_2). Oxygen (O_2) would have been present in very low concentrations.

Oxygen is absent from volcanic gases, and is present at only very low levels in the atmospheres of other planets.

■ When did significant levels of oxygen begin to accumulate in the Earth's atmosphere?

☐ Around 2400 Ma ago (Book 6, Section 3.1).

So an early atmosphere consisting mainly of CO_2 and N_2 and devoid of oxygen is the most likely scenario for the early Earth. There would probably also have been small quantities of other volcanic gases, including sulfur dioxide (SO_2), ammonia (NH_3) and methane (CH_4), and water vapour would certainly have been present. Because oxygen was absent, there would have been no layer of ozone (O_3) in the upper atmosphere of the early Earth.

■ What effect would this have had on the type of solar radiation reaching the Earth's surface?

☐ It would have contained far more short-wavelength radiation (ultraviolet, UV). Radiation with these wavelengths is either completely or largely absorbed by the ozone layer.

UV radiation is potentially very damaging to surface-dwelling or shallow-water organisms – think how sunburnt fair-skinned people can become. This is one of many reasons why the surface of the early Earth would have been extremely inhospitable to life.

What about the early oceans? For a start, we cannot be certain when oceans actually formed. Initially, conditions were probably too hot and the bombardment from space was too intense for oceans to condense. Thus, Zahnle (the author of Article 3) has argued that most of Earth's water was present as steam. The chemical composition of any early oceans is again a matter of guesswork. Modern seawater is salty, i.e. it contains quite large amounts of dissolved ions that come from rocks. Ions in rocks under the sea may pass into solution, and ions from rocks on land can enter rivers that carry them into the oceans. Some of the dissolved ions might also come from the atmosphere: carbon dioxide, sulfur dioxide and hydrogen chloride dissolve in rain and form hydrogen carbonate, sulfate and chloride ions respectively.

One metallic ion which is common in rock minerals, iron, was probably much more abundant in the early ocean than it is today – perhaps 1000 times more so. Iron has two principal ionic forms (Book 6, Section 3.1), Fe^{2+} and Fe^{3+}. In

Book 4, Section 8.3, you learnt that oxidation is the loss of electrons. By losing an electron, an Fe^{2+} ion can be converted into an Fe^{3+} ion:

$$Fe^{2+} \xrightarrow{\text{oxidation}} Fe^{3+} + e^-$$

The reverse of this reaction is reduction, in which an Fe^{3+} ion gains an electron:

$$Fe^{3+} + e^- \xrightarrow{\text{reduction}} Fe^{2+}$$

Fe^{2+} is readily converted into Fe^{3+} under oxidising conditions; in addition, Fe^{2+} compounds are generally soluble in water whereas relatively few Fe^{3+} compounds have this property.

■ Which form of iron would have been present in the early oceans, and why was it more abundant than it is today?

☐ Fe^{2+}, the reduced form of iron, would have been present, because any Fe^{3+} that formed would have precipitated out as insoluble compounds. Fe^{2+} was more abundant than it is today because there was no oxygen or other oxidising agent to convert it into Fe^{3+}.

The present-day oceans contain relatively little iron because Fe^{3+} can now readily form and be precipitated. The appearance of oxygen in the Earth's atmosphere about 2400 Ma ago led to the first formation of abundant quantities of Fe^{3+}. Remember that you added this date to Figure 2.1.

Volcanic eruptions under the sea were probably more frequent on the early Earth than today, and were another factor influencing the chemical composition of the oceans. Of particular significance (as you will see later) were hydrothermal vents, similar to those described in Book 2 Section 7.3, where hot water gushes out, saturated with minerals and with gases such as methane and carbon dioxide.

The picture of the early oceans emerging from this discussion is of a fairly salty environment with very high levels of reduced iron, Fe^{2+}, and local chemical hot spots associated with volcanoes and hydrothermal vents. Additionally, the heavy bombardment of Earth from space might have significantly affected the composition of the oceans.

2.3.4 Earth's early climate

As mentioned in Section 2.3.1 and as you found in Activity 2.4, for the first 1000 Ma or so of its life (4600–3600 Ma ago) Earth was a turbulent place. The early bombardment would have been particularly heavy 4600–4200 Ma ago. But what was the climate like, especially the temperature, over the period 4200–3400 Ma, when life is thought to have appeared?

■ Think back to Book 1. What is the *primary* energy input that determines the Earth's GMST (global mean surface temperature) today?

☐ Solar radiation absorbed by the surface – this is the radiation intercepted by the Earth (the solar constant times the area), less the amount reflected back to space (specified by the planetary albedo; Book 1 Section 4.3).

(There is also radiation emitted by the atmosphere – this determines the size of the greenhouse effect, which depends on the amounts of greenhouse gases in the atmosphere. This radiation is derived from solar radiation.) If our Sun behaves like other, similar stars, then 4000 Ma ago it would have emitted 20–30% less energy than it does today (Book 1 Section 8.2.2). The distance of the Earth from the Sun has not changed significantly, and therefore the solar constant would have been much lower. Under today's conditions, this would mean a GMST well below 0 °C, with all surface water frozen solid. That in turn would give a high surface albedo because ice reflects solar radiation very effectively, so these two factors would have tended to make Earth a very cold place indeed.

However, other factors might have countered this cold scenario. First, the Earth's interior was much hotter than it is today and heat was being released from it at a greater rate; this would have made the ocean floor warmer but probably had little effect on surface temperatures. Second, there were all those impacts from space, which generated a great deal of heat. Third, and potentially of greatest significance, there was probably a much stronger greenhouse effect than today.

■   Why would the greenhouse effect have been stronger?

☐   Because of the large atmospheric quantities of CO_2, which is a powerful greenhouse gas.

A fourth factor is that cloud cover might have been greater than it is today, because of the high water vapour content of the atmosphere. Although clouds reflect solar radiation back into space and thus increase the albedo of the early Earth, water vapour is a powerful greenhouse gas. The overall effect of increased cloud cover would act to increase GMST. As shown in Figure 2.7, over the first 1000 Ma of Earth's history, the temperature changed dramatically. It finally settled at a temperature close to today's GMST. This is in accordance with the thinking of most scientists who have worked on this problem, concluding that the warming and cooling factors roughly balanced out and that the Earth around 3600 Ma ago had much the same average temperature as today.

2.4   How did life appear?

The scene is now set for progress towards understanding the origin of life. We have some idea of when life appeared on Earth and of conditions at that time, but the questions of how and where it happened still remain. These two questions are bound very closely together; in this section, you will consider a mechanism for how life might have appeared.

The most widely accepted general mechanism for the origin of life is that living cells were organised from non-living organic molecules such as lipids (fatty substances), proteins and nucleic acids (Book 4, Chapter 15 and Book 5, Chapter 5) which had themselves evolved from simpler precursors by a process called **chemical evolution**, which you will meet again in Section 2.4.1. If this explanation is valid, then we must consider where the simple precursor molecules came from. Were they present on the Earth when it formed?

If you think about the time of the formation of the Earth, you should remember that 4600 Ma ago, the Earth's surface was molten, and volatile species (those that are easily vaporised, such as water) were not stable.

■ Were all of Earth's volatiles driven away when the surface was molten?

□ No – it is thought that the earliest atmosphere contained CO_2 which, as the Earth cooled, would have become incorporated in rocks.

In Section 2.3.1, mention was made of the bombardment of Earth by comets, asteroids and dust. These entities are often rich in organic compounds, as well as water (either as ice, in the case of comets, or bound in minerals in asteroids and dust). So it is probable that the building blocks of life were a combination of material already in the Earth mixed with material delivered by comets, asteroids and dust.

You should note that the discussion here concerns chemicals being delivered to Earth, and not living microorganisms; the latter is a theory called panspermia, and is considered later. Section 2.2 discussed the evidence for the earliest life on Earth. Section 2.3 considered what surface conditions were like before this time. You should have marked the earliest date for which we have evidence for life on Figure 2.1.

■ From Figure 2.1, how much time was probably available for chemical evolution?

□ It was suggested earlier that life had appeared by about 3400 Ma ago. The Earth originated around 4600 Ma ago. That leaves around 1200 Ma for chemical evolution. But remember that Earth's surface was too unstable (because of the heavy bombardment) for life to become established until at least 3800 Ma ago.

It took about 700 Ma from the supposed origin of life (3400 Ma ago) to the appearance of eukaryotic cells with a nucleus (2700 Ma ago); and multicellular animals were not abundant until a further 2100 Ma had elapsed – 610 Ma ago.

2.4.1 Chemical evolution

In the early 1950s, Stanley Miller carried out a series of what were to become classic experiments that influenced theories on the origins of life for decades. These were briefly referred to in Article 2, which you read as part of Activity 2.3. Miller took mixtures of gases (ammonia, methane and hydrogen) and passed an electric current through them. Eventually, a tar-like deposit formed that was found to be a mixture of more complex organic species. These had been built up from the simple gas molecules present at the start of the experiment.

From these experiments, it was assumed that the first steps in chemical evolution must have taken place in the atmosphere, which (in the 1950s) was thought to contain substantial amounts of ammonia, hydrogen and methane. In such an atmosphere, which is strongly reducing, i.e. it tends to promote reduction reactions (Book 4 Section 8.3), UV radiation from the Sun and electrical discharges from lightning can provide the energy necessary to produce a wide array of simple organic building blocks, such as amino acids. These would then have entered the oceans in rain and accumulated there.

Unfortunately for this early hypothesis, the atmosphere was probably not strongly reducing, but is more likely to have been predominantly nitrogen and carbon dioxide, as described in Section 2.3.3 and in Activity 2.3, so the hypothesis that the first stages of chemical evolution took place in the atmosphere had to be discarded.

There have been many other hypotheses, including arguments that reactions occurred on the surfaces of particles of pyrite (iron sulfide) blasted into a steamy atmosphere by the early heavy bombardment. Other people have suggested that scums at the ocean surface, shallow pools, or the surface of clay particles in pools provided suitable sites. Reduced iron, Fe^{2+}, might have played an important role, reducing CO_2 in the presence of UV radiation and water to formaldehyde (CH_2O), which is a useful precursor to several more complex organic molecules, including sugars. Note that water, either as a reactant or as a liquid medium, is essential for all steps in chemical evolution.

As a starting point, assume that simple building blocks (such as methane (CH_4), ammonia (NH_3) and carbon monoxide (CO)) were formed, and move on to the next problem, which is one of concentration, and the chemical reaction known as hydrolysis (Book 4, Section 15.1.2). For simple building blocks to react further to produce larger molecules, especially polymers, the reactant molecules must be quite concentrated to increase the reaction rate. And if the products are not to break down by reacting with water (the hydrolysis reaction), they must be held in some special environment. The solid surface of rocks or clay particles provides one such environment because not only do such surfaces seem to promote polymerisation reactions, they also protect the reaction products. This is why several hypotheses focus on solid surfaces as the site of chemical evolution. You will consider this in Activity 2.5.

Activity 2.5   Polymerisation on the rocks

We expect this activity will take you approximately 15 minutes.

Article 4 is extracted from a book called *Genesis: The Scientific Quest for Life's Origin* by Robert Hazan (2005). The author is an astrobiologist, working as a research scientist in the Geophysical Laboratory of the Carnegie Institution in Washington, DC. He is also Professor of Earth Sciences at George Mason University, Virginia. Hazan is not just a scientist, he is also well-known as a communicator of science and, as this extract shows, his style is informal and pacy.

In Article 4, Hazan describes events leading to the discovery that clay minerals can act as a surface on which small molecules can gather and react to form more complex molecules. He mentions work by several groups of scientists over 50 years of investigation. The author shows how gradually, as results from different experiments are obtained, ideas develop until the picture of an entire process emerges. One of the things that you should note about this extract is that there are no references to specific articles contained within the text, although the author refers to colleagues and the work that they have done. At the back of Hazan's book, however, there are notes associated with each chapter, referring to published articles, and a list of these articles is then gathered together in a bibliography. This is a different style of referencing from that which you have already met, but is appropriate for this type of publication.

As you read the extract, concentrate on sorting out first what James Ferris and his colleagues discovered, and what extra experiments Leslie Orgel and his co-workers performed that supported the idea that solid surfaces were important during chemical evolution. You will then be asked to complete tasks related to this. Note that monomers (from the Greek for 'single part') are single molecules, whereas polymers (from the Greek for 'many parts') consist of many molecular units joined together.

The extract mentions several different chemicals (such as imidazole); don't worry about these – in this case it is the overall picture that is important, not the specific details. After reading the article, carry out the tasks below which give you practice at extracting information. Have a quick look at the tasks now so that you can make notes as you read.

Task 1

Explain, as if to other students who have not read Article 4, what experiments Ferris and colleagues carried out (try to summarise the results in two or three sentences).

Task 2

Describe the significance of Orgel's results in the context of explaining the origin of life. (*About 100 words*.)

You should now read Article 4, consider your responses to the two tasks and then compare your answers with those in the comments on this activity at the end of this book.

Article 4   *Genesis: The Scientific Quest for Life's Origin*

Robert Hazan

Extract

Research by NASA-sponsored teams in California and New York has demonstrated that a variety of layered minerals can adsorb and assemble a variety of other organic molecules. In a *tour de force* series of experiments during the past two decades, chemist James Ferris and colleagues at Rensselaer Polytechnic Institute induced clays to act as scaffolds in the formation of RNA, the polymer that carries the genetic message enabling protein synthesis.

Ferris relied on the simplest of procedures. First, he prepared a solution of "activated" RNA nucleotides, each consisting of a ribose sugar bonded to a phosphate and a base, plus a reactive molecule called imidazole that promotes, or "activates", bonding between nucleotides. Such a solution can sit on the lab bench for weeks with little change. But sprinkle in a bit of a suitable clay mineral and the RNA pieces start to link up. In a matter of hours, lengths of 10 nucleotides form. By the end of 2-week experiments, the RPI team produced RNA strands of more than 50 nucleotides. The fine-grained clay particles had induced polymerization by a process not yet fully understood.

Buoyed by the Ferris team's success other origin-of-life researchers tried their hand at other biopolymers. Leslie Orgel, research professor at the Salk Institute for Biological Studies in San Diego, succeeded in forming a variety of proteinlike chains of amino acids up to several dozen molecules long. Orgel and his students discovered that different minerals preferentially select and polymerize different molecules from a water-based solution. By combining the right mineral with the right molecule, they could form polymers at will.

In conjunction with his experiments, Orgel also developed an elegant theory of "polymerization on the rocks," in which he pointed out both the promise and problems with mineral surfaces. Minerals such as clays and hydroxides certainly can adsorb interesting biomolecules, he noted, including the amino acids and nucleotides essential to life. Furthermore, once two of these molecules are adsorbed close to each other, they have a tendency to bond. As more and more molecules are added to a lengthening polymer, however, the strand becomes more and more tightly bound to the mineral surface. How, he asks, can a polymer contribute to life if it's stuck to the rocks?

One possible answer came from the Harvard University laboratory of geneticist Jack Szostak, who mixed together clays, RNA nucleotides and lipids in the same experiment. Lo and behold, the clays not only adsorbed RNA, but also hastened the formation of lipid vesicles. In the process RNA-decorated clay particles were incorporated into the vesicles. This spontaneous self-assembly of RNA-containing vesicles, though a long, long way from synthesizing life, is perhaps the closest anyone has come to forming a cell-like entity from scratch.

Suppose that reactions on solid surfaces produced a rich mixture of biopolymers (Book 4 Section 15.1); for example: phospholipids (fatty molecules (lipids) linked to phosphate groups, which could spontaneously form a membrane-like structure over the mixture and segregate it more firmly from the surrounding medium); short chains of amino acids (peptides) or even proteins; and simple polynucleotides, the forerunners of nucleic acids. This is still far from being a living cell but it is the sort of system that could have developed during chemical evolution, regardless of whether that evolution occurred on Earth or on another planet. Assume that from such simple beginnings arose the precursors of cells (protocells) from which the first true cells evolved. You will now consider just two important questions about protocells and the first cells: how did they obtain the energy needed to grow and maintain themselves and how did they replicate (i.e. what sort of genetic material did they have)?

2.4.2 The energy question

Early theories about the origin of life assumed that the first cells were heterotrophs.

- ■ Suggest from where the first cells obtained energy if they were heterotrophic (heterotrophs were defined in Book 5, Section 2.3).

- ☐ Heterotrophs (e.g. animals) cannot make sugars (energy) by photosynthesis, and so obtain energy by breaking down complex organic molecules.

For early heterotrophic cells, such molecules would have had to come from the surrounding medium which, according to early theories, was thought to be a kind of soup rich in organic molecules. The energy released would have enabled the formation of complex organic molecules required for growth and maintenance. The scenario just described, based on more recent ideas, does not have a rich organic soup filling the ocean. Increasingly, the balance of opinion has shifted towards the view that the first cells and their immediate precursors (protocells) were autotrophic; that is, they synthesised the large organic molecules that are the basis of life from small inorganic molecules using energy from an external source. **Photoautotrophs** obtain their energy from light, whilst **chemoautotrophs** obtain energy from the oxidation of simple inorganic compounds (such as iron sulfide or hydrogen sulfide) or one-carbon molecules such as methane (CH_4).

The light reactions of photosynthesis (i.e. those that involve a photochemical reaction during which the energy of sunlight is trapped (Book 5 Section 2.3)) might seem horribly complex. The basic process that traps energy is really quite simple; all that is involved is the pumping of hydrogen ions (protons, H^+) across a membrane to create a gradient of concentration and electrical charge. The same basic process operates also in chemoautotrophs. There are modern bacteria living in the Dead Sea and other very salty environments that trap energy using just one protein embedded in their outer membrane which is able to absorb light and pump protons. So it is not beyond the bounds of possibility that the earliest cells and their precursors (protocells) did something similar. If they were at the surface of the Earth they might have used sunlight; if in the depths of the ocean then oxidation of inorganic or simple one-carbon molecules could have been used. For example, hydrogen (H_2) could have been oxidised by transferring two electrons to sulfur (S), producing hydrogen sulfide:

$$H_2(g) + S(s) = 2H^+(aq) + S^{2-}(aq)$$

$$2H^+(aq) + S^{2-}(aq) = H_2S(s)$$

Remember there was no free oxygen to carry out oxidation on the early Earth.

2.4.3 The first genetic material

All organisms today have DNA as their genetic material, as did – it is reasonable to assume – the last universal common ancestor. The problem is that the synthesis of DNA requires the action of several proteins (enzymes), and is chemically difficult. There is much support for the idea that the first genetic material was not DNA but RNA (ribonucleic acid) – protocells might have existed in an **RNA world**. (Remember from Activity 2.5 the type of reactions that RNA could undergo.) In virtually all modern organisms the information in a gene is copied from the DNA to form an RNA molecule. RNA molecules are crucial for the process of protein synthesis in cells. The idea of an RNA-only world is not pure speculation but is based on a respectable body of evidence and, for interest only, some of the evidence is listed below (Table 2.2).

Table 2.2 Evidence supporting the view that RNA was the first genetic material.

Item	Evidence
1	RNA can have catalytic activity, acting like an enzyme.
2	DNA building blocks (deoxyribonucleotides) are synthesised from RNA building blocks, rather than by an independent pathway, suggesting that RNA came first.
3	Some viruses use RNA as their genetic material and could be molecular fossils of the RNA world.
4	RNA plays a central role in several key processes, including protein synthesis.

By far the most dramatic evidence is item 1 in Table 2.2. The catalytic role of RNA is probably a new idea for you and was a great surprise to the scientific world. Its two discoverers, Sidney Altman and Thomas R. Cech, were awarded a Nobel Prize in 1989. Catalytic RNAs, or **ribozymes** (not ribosomes), have been shown to catalyse, for example, the breakdown of proteins, and the assembly of amino acids into rudimentary peptides (proteins). In 1996 an artificial ribozyme (i.e. one created in the laboratory and not one isolated from an organism) was shown to catalyse synthesis of RNA. So perhaps RNA really could have performed two roles essential for life: carry information encoded in its own nucleotide sequence (the genetic role); and catalyse the reactions, including the assembly of proteins (a role now carried out almost exclusively by proteins).

Even this RNA-based system is remarkably complex, however, and it is widely thought that RNA took over the role of information storage from some earlier system. There is no consensus about what this earlier system might have been but, for example, a template based on clay minerals, capable of replication and carrying information, is one suggestion. This is a different role for the clay minerals from that found in Activity 2.5, where the clay simply acted as a catalyst for conversion of simple molecules (monomers) into polymers. The RNA-based system was in turn replaced by one in which DNA became the sole genetic material, leaving to RNA the roles concerned with protein synthesis.

2.5   Where did life first appear?

In the last section, we saw that life formed from simple molecules that, through a series of reactions possibly catalysed by mineral surfaces, eventually became more complex molecules that ultimately developed into DNA. This chain from chemistry to biology does not indicate where the reactions took place, and that question forms the subject matter of this section.

Where did life first appear on Earth? Was it at the surface in a *warm little pond* as described in a letter by Charles Darwin, the great scientist who first proposed a detailed theory of evolution in his classic text, *On the Origin of Species*? Or could it have been in the deep oceans, around hydrothermal vents? Or did life originate elsewhere in the Solar System, being delivered to Earth by comets or asteroids? All these hypotheses have been considered in greater or lesser detail over the years.

2.5.1 The Earth's surface

As you saw in Section 2.4.1, it was thought for many years that life had started in the atmosphere, and then rained down onto the Earth's surface. There then came a majority view amongst scientists that it was more likely that life got going in water at the surface. The main reasoning behind the surface origin theories was that the base of the terrestrial food chain required photoautotrophs, i.e. sunlight was necessary for life to survive. It was also recognised, though, that there were problems associated with a surface origin if life was formed by the build-up of complex molecules from simple starting materials.

■ What problems might be encountered on the surface that would prevent life starting up?

☐ UV radiation from the Sun is more likely to break molecules down rather than build them up. Furthermore, if life were to get going in an ocean (or even a pond), then the concentration of starting materials would have to be very high to give them a chance to interact.

The recognition that clay minerals could act as catalysts for polymerisation of molecules, as a protection from UV radiation and also as a substrate on which molecules could aggregate, were findings that helped explain a surface origin. However, in parallel with understanding of the role that clays played in the origin of life came the discovery in the 1970s of hydrothermal vents, where life was based on chemical, rather than photosynthetic, energy.

2.5.2 The deep ocean

Molten rock wells up and forms new oceanic crust at spreading centres along ocean floor mid-ocean ridges (Book 2 Chapter 2). Hydrothermal vents were discovered close to these areas in the late 1970s. The vents, or 'black smokers', are hot springs where super-heated water (up to 350–400 °C), rich in H_2, CH_4 and H_2S, shoots up from the sea floor (Figure 2.8a). Where the hot water meets the cold oxygen-rich bottom water, there is an instant chemical reaction and sulfides precipitate out from the water, colouring it black. The sulfides build up rapidly to form 'chimneys' reaching heights of several tens of metres.

Discovery of the vents revealed that, despite the depth and darkness, parts of the ocean floor are home to an unusual collection of animals such as clams, mussels and tubeworms (Figure 2.8b), feeding on the Bacteria and Archaea that flourish in these very hot conditions.

The discovery of a successful ecosystem based on chemical energy rather than photosynthesis has raised the possibility that life may not have arisen in surface waters, as original theories suggested. Discovering communities entirely supported by chemoautotrophs has given the impetus to the search for life in other deep oceans, especially on Jupiter's satellite, Europa, where a liquid water ocean is thought to occur below the visible crust of ice (Section 3.2.3).

(a) (b)

Figure 2.8 Hydrothermal vents on the ocean floor. (a) Three 'chimneys' or black smokers; (b) vent fauna that live around the chimneys include tubeworms, clams and mussels.

2.5.3 An extraterrestrial origin for life?

An alternative view to chemical evolution is that of **panspermia**, in which life had an extraterrestrial origin and reached Earth from space, carried by comets, asteroids or dust particles. Although the majority view still favours chemical evolution, some scientists have an open mind on the question.

The astronomer Sir Fred Hoyle (1915–2001) resolutely maintained that an extraterrestrial origin for life must be the case because it was just too unlikely that chemical evolution could have led to life on Earth in the time available.

■ Does the reassessment of the age of the first traces of life increase or decrease the length of time available for chemical evolution to occur?

☐ It increases the time available. In Activity 2.2, you read that there had been a claim that traces of life had been found in rocks around 3850 Ma old. Given that Earth formed 4600 Ma ago, that only left 750 Ma years to progress from a molten Earth to an inhabited Earth (even though by bacteria). It is now thought that the first indisputable traces of life are in rocks 3400 Ma old, a period of 1200 Ma since the formation of the Earth.

However, it is still not known how rapidly chemical evolution occurred. Just because no fossil (chemical or biological) traces of life before 3400 Ma ago have been found, it does not necessarily mean that life did not exist before that time – it may just mean that it hasn't been found yet!

An argument against an extraterrestrial origin has been that no living organism could survive the extreme cold and high radiation environment of outer space, nor the trauma of descent through the Earth's atmosphere and the explosive impact at the surface. When a large object travelling very fast enters the Earth's atmosphere, there is friction with the atmosphere that generates a great deal of heat (Book 3, Section 6.2). This is why the return module of a spacecraft has a robust heat shield and why meteoroids streaking through the atmosphere are seen as bright meteors – they are glowing hot and heat the atmosphere along their paths. Surely, it is argued, any living cells on the surface of such bodies would be burnt up during their descent or destroyed in the gigantic explosion when an extraterrestrial body impacts Earth. Against this argument, three points can be made:

1   The interiors of freshly fallen meteorites are known to be cold – only the surface is heated during passage through the atmosphere. On impact, the typical meteorite might break into pieces, but would not be vaporised, and so any organisms in the interior could survive.

2   Minute particles of dust constantly reach Earth from space. Because they are so small, the temperature rise in the slower-moving ones as they travel through the Earth's atmosphere is much less than it is for larger objects – they are rapidly decelerated and then float gently downwards. Perhaps some heat-resistant forms of life (such as spores) could be associated with such particles.

3   Single-celled organisms could be ejected from a planet into space as a result of violent explosions – from volcanoes or meteorite impacts, for example. It has been suggested that they could then be propelled through space by the radiation emitted from stars. A group of Canadian scientists proposed that such radiation-driven life could survive the hostile environment of space for millennia if it were covered by a thin layer of carbon – a sort of protective dust jacket. Frictional heating on re-entry to a planetary atmosphere would then have to be sufficient to fracture this dust jacket (so that the organisms could start functioning again) but not so great as to burn them up completely.

So, although it is still a minority view, consideration is given by some scientists to a possible extraterrestrial origin for life on Earth.

2.6   Where do we find life on Earth today?

So far, the origin of life on Earth has been considered, and life's origins have been traced through a series of chemical reactions that took place once the Earth had cooled sufficiently for water to condense. If we now look at life on Earth today, we can see that it has spread rapidly to fill almost every possible niche. In order to consider where life might exist beyond the Earth, it is a useful process to look at exactly where on Earth life can survive, and the types of organisms that exist. In this way, we can be guided in our search for life beyond Earth (still assuming, though, that any extraterrestrial life is based on the same principles as terrestrial life).

The limits within which life can survive, grow and evolve are its biological envelope. These limits are based on the physical properties of the compounds that make up organisms, and the parameters of the biological envelope guide the search for life elsewhere in the Solar System. In the time between the emergence of life (3400 Ma ago) and the present day, microorganisms have colonised every habitat on Earth in which it is possible for life to survive. Those that exist in the most extreme physical environments are known as **extremophiles**.

The conditions under which different groups of extremophiles survive are described as follows:

Thermophiles and **hyperthermophiles** are found all over the world. Thermophiles typically flourish at temperatures between 50–70 °C whilst hyperthermophiles prefer temperatures as high as 80–110 °C.

■ What genetic evidence is there that is consistent with the idea that a likely site for the origin of life was around hydrothermal vents, where temperatures in excess of 100 °C have been measured?

☐ Many of the microorganisms (especially Archaea) that have the most ancient origins are extreme thermophiles, living in very hot conditions (Figure 2.5). Perhaps, therefore, the universal common ancestor was a thermophile that lived in the hot water around hydrothermal vents.

However, hot places may also occur elsewhere on the Earth – in surface pools close to volcanoes, for example – so thermophile behaviour in ancient organisms does not *necessarily* mean that life originated close to hydrothermal vents.

Psychrophiles are cold-loving organisms that flourish at around 0 °C. The limit for growth is the freezing point of water, so that in briny solutions (which freeze at temperatures below 0 °C), these microorganisms can metabolise at temperatures as low as −20 °C.

Acidophiles are frequently sulfur-loving thermophilic or hyperthermophilic organisms. They metabolise by oxidising sulfur into sulfuric acid and survive down to pH values near 0. In contrast, **alkalophiles** thrive at pH values greater than 7 and up to 12.5.

Halophiles are adapted to survive in liquids with high salt concentrations (about ten times higher than normal seawater) and many organisms within this group are also alkalophiles.

It is clear that microorganisms have colonised every possible habitation on Earth, from the deepest and darkest oceans, to the hottest and most acid of volcanic lakes.

This is as far as this book will go in the story of life's origin on Earth. It is still a very incomplete story, with precious little evidence and much use of imagination ('speculative hypotheses' in science). You might ask 'why bother?' Does it matter if we do not understand how life arose on Earth? To scientists driven by curiosity, yes, it does matter; this is the stuff of pure science and scientists all over the world are beavering away trying to firm up those speculative hypotheses. There is also the more pragmatic point that scientists will be better able to seek out life on other planets, or evidence that life once existed there, if they know how life emerged on Earth.

Activity 2.6   The origin of life on Earth

We expect this activity will take you approximately 40 minutes.

Towards the end of this book (in Activity 5.1) you will be asked to write an extended account (500–600 words). In this activity, you are going to *plan* that account, which will be based on the following question:

> What are the various means by which life might have originated on the Earth?

You have been provided with advice on planning a scientific account in various places in the course, and you may wish to look back at some of this advice now. In particular, you may find it useful to look back to Activities 7.3, 11.1 and 15.1 in Book 5. Note that the question is about the means by which life might have originated, so you are not expected to include when life originated or the environmental conditions at the time. First, skim through Chapter 2 of this book, including the articles, noting down relevant points and the section numbers or articles where you found these points. Don't be tempted to make your notes too detailed at this stage; your aim should be to jot down the main ideas, and you would go back to the section or article for more detail at the stage when you were producing a full draft of the account. Then put the points in a logical order and group them into (what would become) paragraphs. These paragraphs would form the main body of your account. Note, it is appropriate to compare the various ideas, i.e. to highlight the differences and similarities between them, so part of your planned account should do this. You should also think about how you might refer to the sources of information that you use in your account. Finally, it is suggested that you draft the introduction and the conclusion to your planned account – a few sentences for each should be sufficient. The introduction should 'set the scene' and explain your approach to the topic. The conclusion should summarise your main points and emphasise how they address the initial question. No new material should be introduced. Don't forget that if you were writing the full account, you would need to list the references in full at the end of your work.

Now compare your work with the plan prepared by a member of the course team in the comments on this activity at the end of this book.

2.7   Summary of Chapter 2

Life on Earth originated from a universal common ancestor which had almost certainly appeared by 3400 Ma ago. This first life would have been a single-celled prokaryote whose basic requirements were liquid water, a suitable source (or sources) of energy, and chemical raw materials from which to build new cells.

Evidence about the time of life's origin is geological. Zircon grains in metamorphosed rocks indicate that the Earth's surface was stable possibly as early as 4360 Ma ago, and almost certainly by 4100 Ma. Fossil stromatolites show that cyanobacteria-like organisms were in existence 3400 Ma ago, and trace chemicals in rocks suggest that eukaryotes had appeared by around 2700 Ma ago.

Genetic evidence about the nature of the first life is based on comparisons of nucleic acid sequences. Three domains evolved from the universal common ancestor: the Archaea, the Bacteria (which include the cyanobacteria) and the Eukarya from which eukaryotic cells evolved later. These domains must have originated before 3400 Ma ago.

Conditions on the early Earth were influenced strongly by bombardment from space. This had three effects relevant to the origin of life:

1   Before at least 4100–4360 Ma ago conditions were too unstable to support life.

2   Comets impacting on Earth could have contributed significant amounts of water to the early oceans and atmosphere.

3   Impacting comets and asteroids might have contributed organic molecules to Earth.

The early atmosphere was not only derived from impacting bodies but also from outgassing of the Earth's interior by volcanoes. It consisted largely of carbon dioxide, nitrogen and water vapour. There was no oxygen and hence no ozone layer, and so much more UV radiation reached the Earth's surface than does at present.

Oceans may have formed by 4100 Ma ago and a best guess is that they were saline, contained high levels of reduced iron, Fe^{2+}, and had hydrothermal vents.

Protocells and the first cells were probably autotrophs. At the ocean surface they could have obtained energy from sunlight as photoautotrophs; deep in the ocean they would have been chemoautotrophs, obtaining energy by oxidising simple molecules such as hydrogen or methane.

The nature of the first genetic material that stored information and allowed protocells to replicate is unknown. It was probably replaced first by RNA, acting as both genetic material and an enzyme (the RNA world), and then by DNA.

However and wherever life originated, it has now spread to occupy habitats with a wide range of environments, from very hot to very cold, acidic, alkaline and saline.

Chapter 3
Life elsewhere in the Solar System

In Book 5 you learned about the diversity of life on Earth. This is a subject about which a lot is known – and yet the *origin* of life is not fully understood, as you saw in the previous chapter. What *is* known is something of the development and evolution of life on Earth. The relevant information comes not only from the fossil record but also from the genetic evidence found in the nucleic acids of individual species. Living things on Earth have a range of characteristics from highly evolved beings like ourselves, to the primitive organisms from which all life evolved. So, when 'life elsewhere in the Solar System' is discussed, this does not necessarily mean entities that we could talk to, or otherwise communicate with ('little green men'). It doesn't even mean to imply life forms that would be easily visible, or display obvious movement over distances visible to the naked eye. It simply means single-celled organisms that would be analogous to prokaryotes.

Why just prokaryotes? The reason is that on Earth there is evidence for the continuous existence of single-celled organisms from the time of life's first appearance on the planet (3400 Ma ago). In other words, even though there are bacteria on the Earth *today*, they represent a very primitive class of organism. In contrast, other primitive entities (such as algae, slimes, moulds, etc.) are more evolved than bacteria, having first formed later in geological time. The great antiquity of bacteria should be contrasted with the length of time that human beings have been in existence. In Book 6, Figure 3.21, you saw that our own species, *Homo sapiens*, has only been around for about 0.15 Ma. If you imagine (as you did in the question at the end of Section 2.2.1) that all of geological time (4600 Ma) is scaled to a 24-hour day, this is equivalent to only about the last 3 seconds!

Bacteria might not be obviously visible, but it should be realised that on the present-day Earth such organisms are extremely widespread and contribute to a large part of the biomass. Indeed, bacteria are found inside humans and other animals, within oilfields, deep within the Earth's crust, in soil and so on. If life evolved elsewhere in the Solar System, it might well have originated in a broadly similar manner to that on Earth. In other words, primitive life forms on other worlds might well share characteristics with certain terrestrial bacteria; although life could have evolved elsewhere beyond the bacterial stage, the discussion here is confined to the most primitive forms.

It has to be pointed out that at the moment there is currently *no* conclusive proof of the existence of life today anywhere in the Solar System, other than on Earth. At the very least, though, there might be environments out there of a sort no longer present on Earth but which might help us to piece together a general picture of planetary development. This then might help us to understand the conditions that allowed the origin and evolution of life on Earth and possibly elsewhere. A greater hope is that within the Solar System we shall be able to find the fossilised remains of an environment within which the most primitive of life forms were just beginning to evolve. Such a find might be the 'missing link' in our quest to understand the origin of life on Earth. The greatest hope is that a biosphere will be found.

It is quite possible to be led, rather rapidly, down paths that are pure science fiction. So in order to prevent this, this chapter will take the characteristics and habitats of life on Earth as a framework within which to consider where life might exist beyond Earth. What is needed is a study and evaluation of the various habitats within the Solar System that *could* conceivably support life now, or that could have done so in former times. This chapter will concentrate on two possible candidates for places where scientists think there is at least a possibility that life may once have evolved (or might even exist today). The bodies concerned are the planet Mars and one of Jupiter's large satellites, Europa. Also considered will be the largest satellite of Saturn, Titan, not as a habitat for life, but as a place where prebiotic (i.e. before life) chemistry might have occurred.

But first, in Section 3.1, some of the other bodies of the Solar System will be examined and the likelihood of them supporting life will be evaluated. This should give you an insight into how scientists approach an intellectual challenge. Before you continue, you might want to refresh your memory concerning the general layout of the Solar System (see Figure 3.1, and also Book 2 Section 11.1).

3.1   A quick assessment

First consider what is required for life (at least as currently understood in a terrestrial context).

■ What three conditions necessary for terrestrial life were noted in Chapter 2?

☐ (i) Liquid water, to act as a solvent and a reactant; (ii) light, or other types of electromagnetic radiation, or chemical energy, to construct large molecules; (iii) supplies of the chemicals (atoms, ions or molecules) needed to construct living cells.

It is also likely that a surface of some kind is needed – particularly a solid surface, even if it is under an ocean. Central to the issue of where to look is the requirement for liquid water, which has to be kept from escaping to space – in other words, a planetary-sized body. This should not be too small, otherwise its gravity would be too low, and any water present within an atmosphere, or as surface liquid, would be lost to space. For a rocky body, the radius needs to be at least about 10^3 km. Alternatively, liquid water could be retained under a sealing layer of ice. Even if a planetary body is sufficiently large, the surface temperature must be suitable for water to be able to exist in the liquid state (between 0 and 100 °C). Atmospheric pressure also has to be sufficiently high, or liquid water will vaporise very quickly. At 0 °C the pressure needs to be at least 600 Pa, and at 100 °C it needs to be at least 10^5 Pa.

Armed with the above criteria you can begin to appraise the habitability of some of the bodies of the Solar System, and decide where *not* to look. It is useful to compare the potential contenders with the Earth, a body that orbits the Sun at a mean distance of 1.50×10^8 km. This is a convenient unit of distance within the Solar System, and it is given a special name – the **astronomical unit** (AU). The Earth is a rocky planet which has liquid water at the surface and an atmosphere.

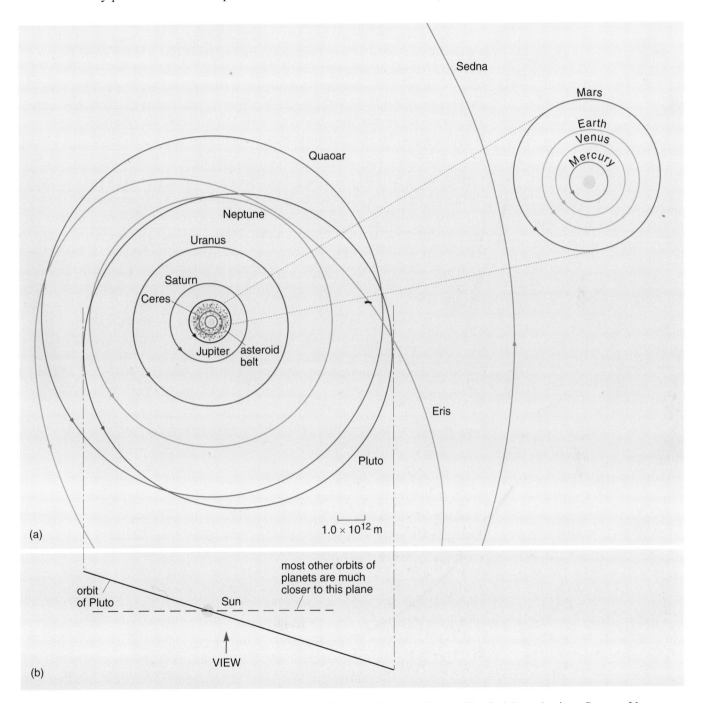

Figure 3.1   The orbits (to scale) of the eight major planets, Mercury, Venus, Earth, Mars, Jupiter, Saturn, Uranus and Neptune; the three dwarf planets, Pluto, Ceres and Eris (Ceres is an asteroid and Pluto and Eris are Kuiper Belt objects); and two other large Kuiper Belt objects (Sedna and Quaoar). Also shown is the asteroid belt lying between Mars and Jupiter. (a) From a viewpoint perpendicular to the Earth's orbit; (b) from edgewise to the Earth's orbit. The average distance from the Earth to the Sun is 1.5×10^{11} m (150 million kilometres). The yellow disc representing the Sun is not to scale.

It has a mean radius of 6371 km and the atmospheric pressure at the surface is about 10^5 Pa. The present global mean surface temperature of the Earth (as you will recall from Book 1) is about 15 °C.

Before you look in some detail at the individual bodies of the Solar System, consider briefly the Moon, which is the Earth's only natural satellite. It orbits at a distance of about 384 000 km from Earth and has a mean radius of 1738 km. Observers of old thought that the dark areas of the Moon's surface were seas – they even called them *mare* (plural, *maria*) from the Latin word for sea. However, as we now know from the *Apollo* and *Luna* missions, the Moon is dry, and always has been – the maria are floods of basalt, not water. In other words, it is unlikely that the Moon could ever have supported life.

That said, there was much excitement following the *Clementine* mission in 1994, when radar data was thought to show that ice was present in permanently shadowed regions in craters at the Moon's south pole. With temperatures never climbing above 90 K (−183 °C), ice would remain frozen and would not sublime (that is, convert from solid to gas without passing through a liquid phase). This report was followed up by the *Prospector* mission, which used a different technique to show that ice seemed to be present at both the north and south poles. When the *Prospector* mission was due to end, the spacecraft was deliberately crashed into one of the potential ice-bearing craters, in the hope that water would be found in the resulting plume of impact ejecta (the rocks and gas thrown out in an impact). Unfortunately, the impact plume was not visible, and so no water was detected. This does not necessarily mean that ice is not present, just that the experiment was not successful.

■ What might be the origin of ice within the lunar soil?

☐ Comets that impacted the lunar surface over its history.

3.1.1 Mercury, Pluto and beyond

This section will start with Mercury, the closest of all planets to the Sun (distance 0.387 AU). It is a small rocky planet (2440 km radius) with no appreciable atmosphere. Since there is no atmosphere, the Sun's UV radiation reaches the surface and would destroy any organic compounds present. Thus, even if some organic materials had been recently added to the surface of Mercury by comets or meteoroids (as was considered in the case of the early Earth; Section 2.3.2), they would relatively quickly have been destroyed by solar radiation.

■ In order to check that you understand the usage of the astronomical unit to express distances, calculate the distance of Mercury from the Sun in kilometres.

☐ The distance from Mercury to the Sun is 0.387 AU.

1 AU = 1.50×10^8 km

so 0.387 AU = $0.387 \times (1.50 \times 10^8)$ km

Thus the distance is 5.81×10^7 km.

As a consequence of its proximity to the Sun, the daytime temperatures at the surface of Mercury reach about 400 °C, whereas the negligible atmosphere leads to the night-time temperatures dropping to −180 °C. The large temperature variation makes it impossible to have liquid water at the surface. Also the lack of appreciable atmospheric pressure rules out liquid water.

■ Does Mercury seem to be habitable?

☐ No. Mercury is not a good place to look for life.

The *Mariner 10* mission of 1974–75 did not orbit the planet, but had three fly-by encounters with Mercury, taking images of only one side of the planet. It was not until January 2008 that NASA's *Messenger* mission (launched in August 2004) swung past Mercury and took close-up images of its surface, including pictures of the side that had not previously been seen (Figure 3.2). *Messenger* settles into its final orbit around Mercury in March 2011. A second mission, *BepiColombo*, is a joint mission between ESA (the European Space Agency) and JAXA (the Japanese Space Agency) and is scheduled for launch in 2013.

At the other extreme, consider the body that, until recently, was considered to be the planet furthest from the Sun – Pluto. Pluto is an icy-rocky body 1137 km in radius, with a low surface temperatures, below −230 °C. Pluto has an extremely thin atmosphere, probably less than 1 Pa, mostly nitrogen (N_2), but with some methane (CH_4) and carbon monoxide (CO). It orbits the Sun once every 248 years. It has a satellite known as Charon, which is about half the radius of Pluto itself. Pluto and Charon are now classed as members of a population known as Kuiper Belt Objects (Book 2 Section 11.1). Currently just over 1000 of these objects have been discovered, but theories of the origin of the Solar System indicate that there are many more, probably over 70 000 with diameters greater than 100 km. An up-to-date list is maintained by the Minor Planet Center (see the link on the course website).

■ As a quick revision, recall from Book 3, Section 6.4, the relationship between the Celsius and Kelvin temperature scales, and express −230 °C in the SI unit of temperature.

☐ To convert a Celsius temperature to the Kelvin scale, 273 must be added to the Celsius value, so −230 °C is equal to (−230 + 273) K, which is 43 K.

These icy-rocky bodies are very 'primitive', representing accumulations of the ices that condensed at the outer regions of the Solar System early in its history. They have a direct association with comets – in fact, some comets are thought to originate in the Kuiper Belt. Because comets are icy bodies that become displaced from their original orbits into ones that bring them closer to the Sun, they can be studied using conventional astronomical techniques. In this way their composition is well understood. For instance, we know that they are made up in part of small rocky dust grains (the 'shooting stars' that you can sometimes see in the night sky are mainly dust from comets, the dust entering the atmosphere so rapidly that it makes the

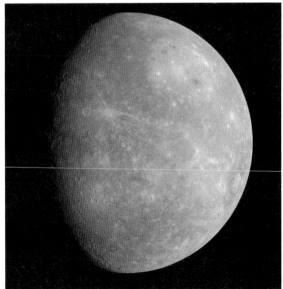

Figure 3.2 The previously unseen side of Mercury as observed by NASA's *Messenger* mission.

atmosphere incandescent). More importantly comets contain organic molecules in abundance. But these are not biologically produced – on the contrary, they were made during abiological (i.e. non-biological) events that have some similarities with the kinds of reactions used for producing polymers and drug molecules that you met in Book 4, Chapters 13 and 16.

As well as conventional astronomical techniques, space probes can also be used to study comets when they enter the inner Solar System. There have been several very successful missions in the past couple of decades, the first of which was an ESA mission known as *Giotto*, which conducted a close fly-by of comet Halley in March 1986.

The spacecraft flew within 600 km of Halley's Comet, and took the first close-up picture of the nucleus (Figure 3.3). Comets were first called 'dirty snowballs' in the 1950s by the astronomer Fred Whipple, reflecting the (then) state of knowledge. The image of icy bodies into which dust was embedded remained until the *Giotto* mission when it was found that comet Halley's nucleus was closer to an 'icy dirtball'. The surface of the comet was dark, composed of organic (i.e. carbon-rich) and silicate particles, rather than bright, as would have been expected if the surface were icy.

Figure 3.3   Nucleus of Halley's comet taken as the *Giotto* mission approached the comet. The nucleus is approximately 15 km across. The Sun is shining from the left, causing warming of the nucleus, and producing jets of dust as the ice vaporises.

The picture of comets as being more rocky than icy has been reinforced by two subsequent cometary missions. The *Deep Impact* mission gathered image and composition data during a fast fly-by a distance of 500 km from comet Tempel 1 after the comet had been hit by a copper projectile. The data showed that the comet surface and ejecta from the impact were mainly rocky dust, with some ice mixed in with the dust.

The *Stardust* spacecraft flew past comet Wild 2 (Figure 3.4a) in January 2004, collecting dust fragments from the comet's tail at a distance of 250 km from the nucleus. The dust was returned to Earth in January 2006, for analysis by scientists around the world (including a team from the Open University). The relative speed between comet Wild 2 and the collector was 6 km s^{-1}. At this speed, any grains hitting a solid surface would be vaporised, and so in order to capture the cometary grains, a special collector had to be built. This is shown in Figure 3.4b. Each of the small compartments, or cells, is filled with aerogel. This is a solid material with a very low density, around 3 kg m^{-3} (remember water has a density of 1000 kg m^{-3}). As the particles penetrated the aerogel, they did not vaporise, but were slowed down and stopped inside the aerogel, from which they could be carefully extracted.

■   *Stardust* returned cometary dust. Why will analysis of dust not give the whole picture about comets?

☐   Comets are mixtures of dust with ice and gas, neither of which were collected by the *Stardust* mission.

Question 3.1

What can be learned from the study of dust from comets?

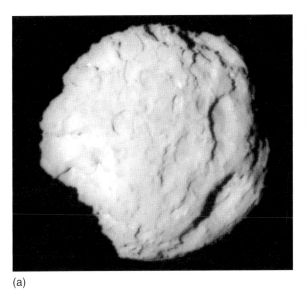

(a)

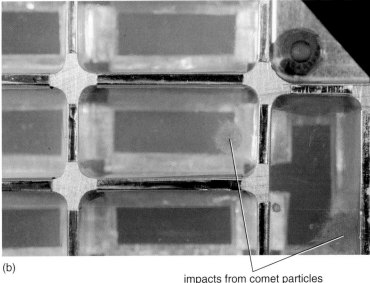

(b)

impacts from comet particles

Figure 3.4 (a) Nucleus of comet Wild 2 from the *Stardust* mission. The nucleus is approximately 5 km across. The spacecraft came within 250 km of the comet, and took this detailed image which shows the rough and cratered surface of the nucleus. (b) Aerogel collector from *Stardust*. Each transparent aerogel cell has dimensions of approximately 5 cm long by 3 cm wide and 2 cm deep. The cells at the centre of the image, and on the lower right-hand side (arrowed) have been hit by cometary dust particles.

Deep Impact and *Stardust* were NASA missions. Europe, through ESA, has a cometary mission in progress: *Rosetta*, which was launched in 2004, will meet up with comet Churyumov–Gerasimenko in 2014. The spacecraft will drop a lander, *Philae*, onto the comet nucleus, where a suite of instruments will analyse the comet. Scientists from the Open University are heavily involved with the mission, and have designed an instrument, called *Ptolemy* that will make in situ measurements of the ices and organic materials using miniaturised versions of instruments that are used routinely in the laboratory. For your interest, further information on the *Rosetta* mission and details of the Open University's involvement can be found by following the link given on the course website.

As you saw in Chapter 2, most scientists recognise that it might have been comets, meteorites, and dust that brought organic compounds to the surface of the early Earth. However, while comets, and by extension Kuiper Belt Objects, are a repository of organic compounds, it requires a relatively warm planetary surface to provide the conditions necessary to allow their development into living entities. Thus, Kuiper Belt Objects, including Pluto, can be ruled out as good places to look for life.

3.1.2 The giant planets and their satellites

Next you will consider the giant planets, i.e. Jupiter, Saturn, Uranus and Neptune. Their mean radii range from 69 910 km (Jupiter) to 24 620 km (Neptune).

Question 3.2

Briefly summarise the internal structures of the giant planets – a simple sketch would be most appropriate. (*Hint*: look back to Book 2 Section 11.2.1.)

The 'gas giants' Jupiter and Saturn are composed predominantly of the elements hydrogen and helium, with relatively small cores. The temperatures at the surfaces of the cores are several thousand degrees, temperatures which are too high for life. As you move outwards from the cores, there is a gradual transition to low-density gases. The temperatures become much lower, but there are no tangible surfaces anywhere, and with no surfaces it is difficult to see how life could originate. Uranus and Neptune are 'gas and ice giants'; like Jupiter and Saturn, they have atmospheres of hydrogen and helium, with traces of water, ammonia and methane. However, the cores of Uranus and Neptune differ from those of Jupiter and Saturn – they have solid rocky cores, overlain by a deep layer of mixed water, methane and ammonia ices.

So, is life on one of the giant planets possible? At face value the answer to this question would appear to be 'no'. And yet, the atmospheres of the planets are not exclusively hydrogen and helium. Indeed, they contain all kinds of complex organic compounds, and water is also present. There could be dust particles in the atmosphere as well. Figure 3.5 shows scars from the impact of a comet (called Shoemaker–Levy 9) onto Jupiter, and comets contain dust. Furthermore, the temperature in the outer atmosphere, at a level where the pressure is a few pascals, is a balmy 0 °C.

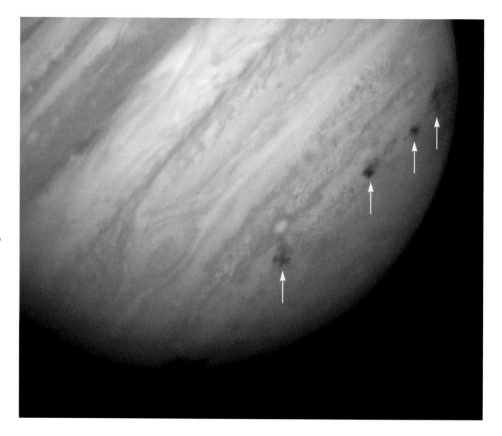

Figure 3.5   Image of Jupiter following impact of fragments of comet Shoemaker–Levy 9. The comet had been broken into several fragments on a previous passage past Jupiter, and the pieces hit Jupiter in a series of collisions over a period of 6 days in July 1994. The scars from the collisions are seen as a series of brown areas in the lower hemisphere of the planet. (Also in the image is the Great Red Spot, a storm that is about the size of the Earth.)

Question 3.3

Do you think it is at least a possibility that life could evolve in the atmosphere of a giant planet like Jupiter? Consider this question with regard to the requirements for life listed at the start of Section 3.1.

The answer to Question 3.3 suggests that, at face value, life is at least possible. But there is a serious problem for any aspiring life forms. Any dust particles would tend to move vertically up and down through the atmosphere. This has the effect that any individual particle would be subject to extreme variations in temperature and pressure, making the evolution or survival of life very unlikely.

So it seems reasonable to proceed on the basis that life on, or within, the giant planets looks unlikely. However, their satellites are a different issue. Each planet has a number of satellites, and there are a few that are relatively large, equivalent in size to Mercury, or to the Earth's Moon, i.e. Ganymede, Callisto, Io, Europa, (all orbiting Jupiter; Figure 3.6a), Titan (orbiting Saturn; Figure 3.6b) and Triton (orbiting Neptune; Figure 3.6c). Thus, in the context of life in the Solar System these bodies should be added to the list of interesting places to consider. All of

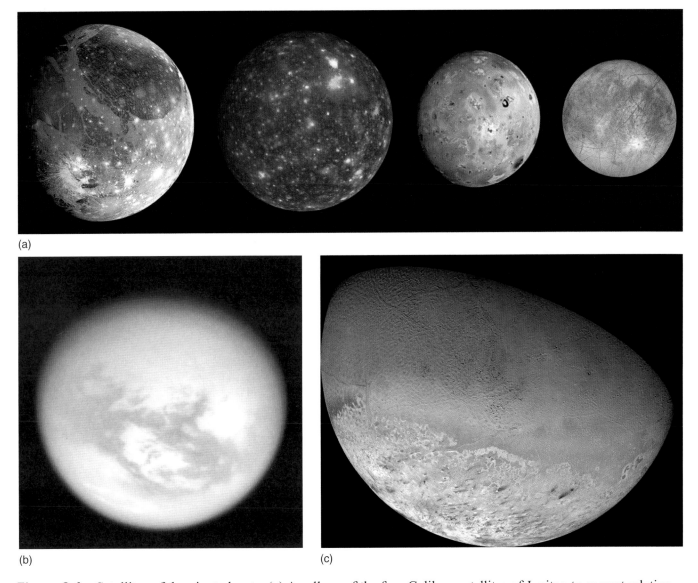

(a)

(b)   (c)

Figure 3.6   Satellites of the giant planets. (a) A collage of the four Galilean satellites of Jupiter, to correct relative sizes. On the far left is Ganymede, then Callisto, Io and Europa; (b) an image taken by the *Cassini* mission of Saturn's largest satellite Titan; (c) an image of part of the surface of Neptune's satellite Triton.

these bodies are fascinating, but Europa and Titan have special characteristics that make them more favourable in origin of life studies. It will not be until spacecraft visit the other bodies and make detailed surveys that we shall have a reliable picture about their potential for supporting life. Titan and Europa are revisited in Section 3.2.

3.1.3 Venus

Now consider some basic facts about Venus. The planet has a radius of 6052 km, so is very similar in size to the Earth, and at 0.723 AU from the Sun is the closest planet to us. The density of Venus is about the same as that of the Earth, and so in terms of bulk chemical composition it is very similar to the Earth. In the light of its proximity to the Earth, and its similar size and density, Venus is often referred to as Earth's 'sister' planet. It is fair to assume that Venus formed from the same kinds of materials as the Earth. Intuitively, you may have expected the environment at the surface of Venus to be similar to that on Earth. And yet it is completely different.

The surface of Venus is a blistering 460 °C, a consequence of a powerful greenhouse effect because the atmosphere is dominantly carbon dioxide (Book 1, Question 5.3 and Book 2, Section 11.2.2). Such temperatures do not allow the survival of liquid water at the surface of the planet. Moreover, the atmosphere itself is very dry – there is very little water vapour. So, why did it all go wrong on Venus?

■　In terms of trying to understand the present-day surface conditions on Venus and Earth, what is the key difference between the two planets that you could imagine might have been contributory?

☐　Venus is closer to the Sun than Earth and so receives correspondingly more solar radiation.

Venus intercepts about twice as much solar radiation as the Earth. If, in the distant past, there was water at the surface of Venus, then it would have evaporated far more readily than water on Earth. In the atmosphere, water is split into hydrogen and oxygen by solar UV radiation, and so the water on Venus was readily exposed to this fate. The hydrogen escaped to space, and the oxygen combined with the surface or with volcanic gases. The absence of oceans on Venus through much or all of its history prevented the formation of carbonate rocks, thus maintaining a high atmospheric content of carbon dioxide and a strong greenhouse effect. The rising surface temperatures drove a lot of carbon out of rocks into the atmosphere to add to the carbon dioxide, and this further increased the greenhouse effect.

The results of these processes are (i) that Venus has an atmosphere mainly of carbon dioxide, with a mass about 100 times that of the Earth's atmosphere, and (ii) that from very early in its history the surface has been very hot. These factors rule out life today and in the past. Furthermore, the atmosphere of Venus contains sulfuric acid rain (although this never reaches the surface because it is too hot). All in all, there are a number of factors that seem to mitigate strongly against life having evolved on Venus.

Apart from the Earth, which are the bodies within the Solar System that might be prime candidates to look for life? None of the planets that we have considered here seem suitable. However, there is one remaining planet, Mars, that we have yet to explore, and it will be considered in the next section. Of the satellites of the giant planets, although several show possibilities, only Titan and Europa will be considered in the next section, because these are the satellites about which we have the most information.

3.2   The prime candidates

Within the Solar System, the prime candidates for extraterrestrial life are Mars, Europa and Titan, and the evidence that can be used to address the question of life on these bodies will shortly be evaluated. Firstly though, consider in a little more detail exactly what it is we are looking for.

Activity 3.1   The search for extraterrestrial life – Part 1

We expect this activity will take you approximately 30 minutes.

Article 5 is extracted from a paper called 'The search for extraterrestrial life', which appeared in the popular scientific magazine *Scientific American* in 1994. Although this article is now a little out of date, it is still one of the best descriptions available of the *Galileo* observations of the Earth.

The article was written by Carl Sagan (1934–1996), at the time a professor of Astronomy and Space Science at Cornell University in the USA. 'The search for extraterrestrial life' is eminently readable, so eventually you may want to read all of it: the paper also includes an excellent description of the biology package experiments carried by the *Viking* landers to Mars, and there is a section towards the end that impinges upon the content of Chapter 4 of this book.

For background information, note that *Galileo* was a spacecraft that explored Jupiter and its satellites between 1995 and 2003. Complicated orbital manoeuvres are often necessary to convey spacecraft around the Solar System. *Galileo* had to go past Venus at one point and past the Earth on two occasions. Sagan considered whether the instruments on Galileo would have been able to detect that Earth was inhabited.

After reading the article, carry out the task below which gives you practice at extracting information. Have a quick look at the task now so that you can make notes as you read.

Task 1

Consider the *Galileo* search for signs of life on Earth. Summarise, in about 200 words, the observations that would have given positive signs of life to an alien studying our planet.

You should now read Article 5, consider your response to the task and then compare your answer with that in the comments on this activity at the end of this book.

Article 5   The search for extraterrestrial life

Carl Sagan

Extract

An observer looking at the data from *Galileo* would immediately notice some unusual facts about the Earth. When my co-workers and I examined spectra taken by *Galileo* at near-infrared wavelengths (just slightly longer than red light), we noted a strong dip in brightness at 0.76 micron, a wavelength at which molecular oxygen absorbs radiation. The prominence of the absorption feature implies an enormous abundance of molecular oxygen in the Earth's atmosphere, many orders of magnitude greater than is found on any other planet in the Solar System.

Oxygen slowly combines with the rocks on the Earth's surface, so the oxygen-rich atmosphere requires a replenishing mechanism. Some oxygen is freed when ultraviolet light from the Sun splits apart molecules of water (H_2O), and the low-mass hydrogen atoms preferentially escape into space. But the great concentration of oxygen (20 percent) in the Earth's dense atmosphere is very hard to explain by this process.

If visible light, rather than ultraviolet, could split water molecules, the abundance of oxygen could be understood, because the Sun emits many more photons of visible light than of ultraviolet. But photons of visible light are too feeble to sever the H–OH bond in water. If there were a way to combine two visible light photons to break apart the water molecule, then everything would have a ready solution. Yet so far as we know, there is no way to accomplish this feat – except through life, specifically through photosynthesis in plants. The prevalence of molecular oxygen in the Earth's atmosphere is our first clue that the planet bears life.

When *Galileo* photographed the Earth, it found unmistakable evidence of a sharp absorption band painting the continents: some substance was soaking up radiation at wavelengths around 0.7 micron (the far red end of the visible spectrum). No known minerals show such a feature, and it is found nowhere else in the Solar System. The mystery substance is in fact just the kind of light-absorbing pigment we would expect if visible photons were being added together to break down water and generate molecular oxygen. *Galileo* detected this

pigment – which we know as chlorophyll – covering most of the land area of the Earth. (Plants appear green precisely because chlorophyll reflects green light but traps the red and blue). The prevalence of the chlorophyll red band offers a second reason to think that the Earth is an inhabited planet.

Galileo's infrared spectrometer also detected a trace amount, about one part per million, of methane. Although that might seem insignificant, it is in startling disequilibrium with all that oxygen. In the Earth's atmosphere, methane rapidly oxidizes into water and carbon dioxide. At thermodynamic equilibrium, calculations indicate that not a single molecule of methane should remain. Some unusual processes (which we know to include bacterial metabolism in bogs, rumina and termites) must steadily refresh the methane supply. The profound methane disequilibrium is a third sign of life on the Earth.

Finally, *Galileo*'s plasma-wave instrument picked up narrow-band, pulsed, amplitude-modulated radio emissions coming from the Earth. These signals begin at the frequency at which radio transmissions on the Earth's surface are first able to leak through the ionosphere; they look nothing like natural sources of radio waves, such as lightning and the Earth's magnetosphere. Such unusual, orderly radio signals strongly suggest the presence of a technological civilization. This is a fourth sign of life and the only one that would not have been apparent to a similar spacecraft flying by the Earth anytime within the past two billion years.

The *Galileo* mission served as a significant control experiment of the ability of remote-sensing spacecraft to detect life at various stages of evolutionary development on other worlds in the Solar System. These positive results encourage us that we would be able to spot the telltale signature of life on other worlds. Given that we have found no such evidence, we tentatively conclude that widespread biological activity now exists, among all the bodies of the Solar System, only on the Earth.

The *Galileo* results obtained from observations of the Earth show us quite clearly that we know how to spot the signs of life from relatively few simple measurements. So far none of the requisite signals from any other bodies in the Solar System have been observed, though scientists are still not 100% sure that life does *not* exist beyond the Earth. They really need to go and visit the various planets and satellites in order to obtain a more conclusive picture.

3.2.1 Titan

Before tackling the various observations of Mars and Europa you will consider Titan (Figure 3.7) – the largest satellite of Saturn. You read in Chapter 2 about some of the ideas regarding the origin of life on Earth, and the fact has been alluded to that our knowledge remains incomplete because of several gaps in the evidential record. Earth harboured life since about 3400 Ma; we assume that this life did not exist prior to the formation of the Earth 4600 Ma ago. The vital period, in which life got started, coincides with a time interval that is only very poorly represented in the geological record on Earth. In order to circumvent this lack of evidence there have been many experiments over the years that attempt to simulate conditions on the early Earth, and there have been many more directed towards assessing how the sub-components of living entities may have formed or evolved. 'Life' has not thus far been re-created from assumed starting materials in a test-tube – but are there other places where the chemistry of life's origins could be studied? The Solar System provides us with many insights into the processes that we seek, and a most appropriate example can be found in Titan.

With a radius of 2575 km, Titan is the second largest satellite in the Solar System (after Jupiter's largest satellite, Ganymede). For comparison, Mercury has a radius of 2440 km and the Earth's Moon 1738 km. What makes Titan so special for our attempts to understand the origin of life on Earth is that it is the only body in the Solar System other than the Earth that has a dense nitrogen atmosphere. The surface atmospheric pressure on Titan is almost one and a half times that on Earth. We know that Titan's atmosphere contains about 95% nitrogen, but no oxygen; it also contains a variety of hydrocarbons, which rain down onto the surface whereupon they may interact with water (following impact events for instance). This natural laboratory may therefore be a very important analogue of the early Earth.

Although very little of the surface can be seen with optical telescopes, we now know more about this interesting place from the *Cassini* spacecraft orbiting around Saturn and more especially from the *Huygens* probe that descended through the atmosphere of Titan on 14 January 2005 (Figure 3.8). Further information about the mission can be found by following the links given on the course website.

Figure 3.7 A view of Titan from a composite of four images taken by the *Cassini* spacecraft from a distance of around 140 000 km in March 2005.

Figure 3.8 Image of Titan's surface from the *Huygens* probe after it landed on 14 January 2005. The 'boulders' in the foreground are probably pebbles of methane ice, and are about 20 cm across.

Activity 3.2   Tuning in to Titan

We expect this activity will take you approximately 40 minutes.

'Tuning in to Titan' is the title of Article 6, about ESA's very successful *Huygens* mission to Titan, the biggest of Saturn's 56 satellites. The author, Jean-Pierre Lebreton, is the mission manager and project scientist of the mission, and in the article he describes the results that came from the probe, both as it descended through Titan's atmosphere, and when it landed. The article was published in the February 2006 edition of *Physics World*, a magazine produced by the UK's Institute of Physics.

You are asked to access the article electronically through the Open University Library website. Follow the link given on the course website for Activity 3.2.

Cassini–Huygens was a joint mission between NASA and ESA to the Saturnian system. The aim of *Cassini* was to acquire images and data of Saturn and its satellites as it orbited through the system. *Huygens* was a lander on Titan. At the time of writing (late 2007), *Cassini* is still returning spectacular images of Saturn, its rings and its moons, such as the one shown in Figure 3.9.

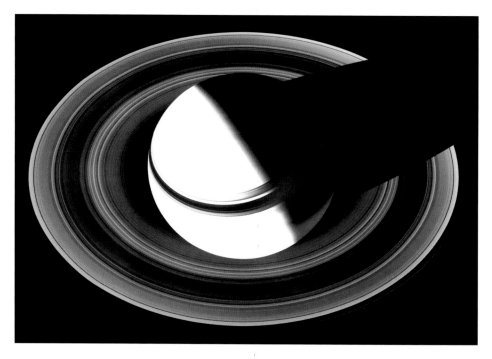

Figure 3.9   A mosaic of 36 images taken over a period of 2.5 hours by the *Cassini* mission combined to produce an image of Saturn's rings. The Sun is shining from the lower left corner of the picture. This has the effect of casting a shadow of the rings onto the bright hemisphere of Saturn, as well as throwing Saturn's shadow across the rings.

The Open University was responsible for one particular experiment, the Surface Science Package (known as SSP), which travelled with the *Huygens* probe down through Titan's atmosphere and made measurements of the physical properties of the satellite's surface. In fact, it was an OU instrument, the penetrometer, that was the first part of *Huygens* to touch the surface. The instrument was designed to penetrate the surface, to see what it was like: hard or soft, icy or granular. The lead scientist on this package, Professor John Zarnecki, described the surface of Titan as having a thin ice crust, with a softer layer below. This was reported as Titan being 'a bit like crème brulée'.

After reading the article, carry out the tasks below which give you practice at extracting information. Have a quick look at the tasks now so that you can make notes as you read.

Task 1

Both the *Voyager* space probe and the Hubble Space Telescope (HST) have taken images of Titan, but before *Huygens* arrived we had no idea what the surface of Titan looked like. Explain why this was the case.

Task 2

Huygens' camera took images of features that looked like rivers. What liquid might have caused them?

Task 3

Outline the main features that make Titan so interesting to astrobiologists who are looking to understand the origin of life on Earth.

You should now read Article 6, consider your responses to the three tasks and then compare your answers with those in the comments on this activity at the end of this book.

3.2.2 Mars

Mars has, for many years, held a special relationship with humankind. Indeed, the planet has featured in many works of fantasy and science fiction, where it is depicted as being inhabited by aggressive and expansionist aliens. Psychologically we are already conditioned to the notion of life on Mars – but what is the reality? Mars is the next planet out from the Sun after the Earth (Figure 3.10), lying at 1.52 AU. It is a rocky body, 3390 km radius, with a thin atmosphere of carbon dioxide, and surface temperatures that can reach up to 20 °C. The surface pressure, however, is close to 600 Pa, the minimum to prevent liquid water from vaporising very rapidly (boiling). There is no evidence of liquid water on Mars today (though there is water ice at or near the surface).

Since 1965, when *Mariner 4* became the first successful mission to Mars, almost 40 spacecraft have been sent to Mars. Approximately 50% of them have failed, either on launch from Earth or on arrival at Mars. Mission success rate is increasing with time, as a very high percentage of the early launches failed. Despite the number of missions, only three spacecraft have been sent with the specific objective of analysing the surface for biological matter. Of the three, the most recent (2003) was ESA's *Beagle 2* lander (designed and built at the Open University, and named after Charles Darwin's ship the *Beagle*). Unfortunately, no signal was received from the spacecraft after it should have landed on Mars in December 2003, and so it is presumed to have crashed.

The two other spacecraft that carried biological experiments were NASA's *Viking 1* and *Viking 2* that were launched separately in 1976. Results from these experiments were ambiguous. They seemed to suggest that chemicals added to Martian soil were metabolised (i.e. indicating the presence of life), but there was no evidence at all for any organic molecules (i.e. no evidence for any living things). These misleading results probably came about because Mars' surface was much more

Figure 3.10   One face of Mars, with the polar caps visible. The image is a true colour image taken by the OSIRIS instrument on ESA's *Mars Express* orbiting spacecraft.

oxidised than had been thought before the *Viking* craft landed. It is now believed that the Sun's radiation destroys any organic compounds present in the top few millimetres of Mars' surface. So to find any signs of carbon-based life, a space mission needs to be able to test materials from below the surface.

How would you test for the presence of life? An alien spacecraft landing on Earth would have no difficulty assessing the presence of life – you have already considered the *Galileo* results that show, from afar, the presence of terrestrial life. But imagine that the alien spacecraft was only fitted with a camera. On the ground it would be fairly easy to observe signs of life with the camera, if it was in the right place. But what if the spacecraft landed in the middle of the Sahara, or in Antarctica? You would argue that it would be unwise to have chosen such locations in the first place. But the *Viking* landers could not have landed just *anywhere*. Their landing sites were chosen partly on the basis of technical considerations – mainly the sites had to be fairly flat, with not too many obvious obstacles that might cause the spacecraft to land awkwardly. More than 20 years later, in July 1997, *Pathfinder* arrived at the planet with the same constraints on landing site selection – in fact *Pathfinder* was put down only a few hundred kilometres from one of the *Viking* sites (Figure 3.11). And of course, it was obvious to scientists in the *Viking* era that Mars was not *teeming* with life. If anything, they supposed that the Martian surface might be analogous to that of, say, the surface of the Earth 4000 Ma ago.

Figure 3.11   Panorama of the surface of Mars taken by the *Pathfinder* mission in 1997, 21 years after the *Viking* missions. This site, where *Pathfinder* landed, has been named after Carl Sagan.

Despite the lack of evidence for life on Mars, the subject is still widely debated. Why is this? It has already been pointed out that advances have been made in understanding the distribution of life on Earth. But this is not the only reason. In the decade since *Pathfinder* landed in 1997, there have been several very successful missions to Mars (*Mars Global Surveyor*, *Mars Express*, *Mars Odyssey*, *Mars Reconnaissance Orbiter*, *Spirit* and *Opportunity*). There have also been several unsuccessful missions as well (*Beagle 2*, *Climate Orbiter*, *Polar Lander*), showing that Mars still keeps its reputation as being a difficult place to visit.

All the recent missions have sent back highly detailed images of Mars' surface. The orbiters have shown places where changes in the landscape look as if they have been caused by recent landslides, implying that water might still be active below the surface. There have been images interpreted as frozen dust-covered former seas, as well as river valleys and gorges. Catalogues of these images can be found by following the links on the course website.

Both NASA and ESA have sent missions to Mars. NASA has a planned programme that aims to 'follow the water' whilst ESA has a programme (*Aurora*) that is designed to lead up to the human exploration of Mars.

■ Why would NASA want to 'follow the water'?

☐ On the assumption that where there is water there is, or might have been, life.

There have been two very successful rovers also exploring the Martian surface. The Mars Exploration Rovers (MER), called *Spirit* and *Opportunity*, were landed at different points on Mars' surface in early 2004. Cameras on the two rovers have taken close-up pictures of the rocks and soil that they have travelled over (Figure 3.12a). Although water hasn't yet been found, *Spirit* and *Opportunity* have both discovered significant indications that water has been present at some point in Mars' history. Instruments on board the rovers detected the mineral jarosite, which contains water as part of its make-up, and which is produced when water runs through basalts. The rovers have found also deposits of 'blueberries', small, round hematite objects (Figure 3.12b) produced by water.

(a)

(b)

Figure 3.12 (a) Panorama of Payson Ridge taken by the Mars Exploration Rover *Opportunity*. The ridge outcrops on one side of the crater 'Erebus' and layered rocks can be seen in the crater wall, which is about 1 m high; (b) close-up image of the hematite 'blueberries' analysed by *Opportunity*. The lighter-coloured circle (5 cm in diameter) is where the surface of the rock has been ground away by the Rock Abrasion Tool – RAT – to show the fresh interior surface.

Despite all the analytical instruments that have gone to Mars, none has yet detected carbon at the surface, or recorded any life forms there. We are left pondering the question of whether life ever got started on Mars. One way in which we can attempt to answer this question is to study Martian meteorites. There are currently around 40 Martian meteorites known, with new samples turning up about once a year. A team of scientists working in the US claimed that they had found a primitive Martian fossil in the Martian meteorite called ALH 84001. You can read about this claim, and about meteorites from Mars in Activities 3.3 and 3.4, respectively.

Activity 3.3   Search for past life on Mars

We expect this activity will take you approximately 15 minutes.

You are about to read two short extracts from an article (Article 7) that was published in the journal *Science*.

You will first read the abstract of the paper (Extract 1). This is what a scientist not working in the area of the paper might glance at to gain an impression of what the paper was about – it represents a short distillation of the paper's content. After reading the abstract you will then look at the last paragraph of the paper (Extract 2), which summarises the main conclusions (a traditional ending to a scientific paper). Figure 3.13 reproduces images of the alleged Martian bacterium and its carbonate host.

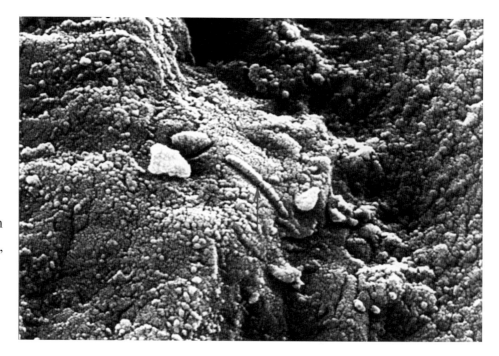

Figure 3.13   A high resolution scanning electron microscope image of a possible 'microfossil' within a patch of carbonate in the ALH 84001 Martian meteorite. The worm-like structure (arrowed) is about 200 nm (0.2 μm) long.

What you need to get out of Article 7 is the conclusion that a Martian meteorite might contain evidence for life on Mars in the distant past. It was a controversial paper that caused much media and public attention. You will notice that there are nine authors – it is often the case that a ground-breaking discovery will involve many scientists working together. It is also testimony to the multidisciplinary nature of some aspects of scientific work (which in the present example involved workers from four separate institutions).

There are some technical terms that require explanation. You met hydrocarbons in Book 4 Section 12.2, and should recall that they are chemical compounds made out of carbon and hydrogen. Polycyclic aromatic hydrocarbons are compounds in which many rings of carbon are joined together. They are often produced by combustion – you will encounter them in the blackened surface of barbecued food!

Scanning electron microscopy (SEM) and transmission electron microscopy (TEM) are types of microscopy that provide very high magnifications and use beams of electrons for 'illumination' rather than light.

After reading the article, carry out the task below which gives you practice at extracting information. Have a quick look at the task now so that you can make notes as you read.

Task 1

Summarise, in your own words, the five lines of evidence, given in the extracts from Article 7, which the authors cite as being compatible with the existence of past life on Mars.

You should now read both extracts, consider your response to the task and then compare your answer with that in the comments on this activity at the end of this book.

Article 7   Search for past life on Mars: possible relic biogenic activity in Martian meteorite ALH84001

David S. McKay, Everett K. Gibson Jr., Kathie L. Thomas-Keprta, Hojatollah Vali, Christopher S. Romanek, Simon J. Clemett, Xavier D.F. Chillier, Claude R. Maechling, Richard N. Zare

Extract 1

Abstract: Fresh fracture surfaces of the Martian meteorite ALH84001 contain abundant polycyclic aromatic hydrocarbons (PAHs). These fresh fracture surfaces also display carbonate globules. Contamination studies suggest that the PAHs are indigenous to the meteorite. High-resolution scanning and transmission electron microscopy study of surface textures and internal structures of selected carbonate globules show that the globules contain fine-grained, secondary phases of single-domain magnetite and Fe-sulfides. The carbonate globules are similar in texture and size to some terrestrial bacterially induced carbonate precipitates. Although inorganic formation is possible, formation of the globules by biogenic processes could explain many of the observed features, including the PAHs. The PAHs, the carbonate globules, and their associated secondary mineral phases and textures could thus be fossil remains of a past Martian biota.

Extract 2

In examining the Martian meteorite ALH84001 we have found that the following evidence is compatible with the existence of past life on Mars: (i) an igneous Mars rock (of unknown geologic context) that was penetrated by a fluid along fractures and pore spaces, which then became the sites of secondary mineral formation and possible biogenic activity; (ii) a formation age for the carbonate globules younger than the age of the igneous rock; (iii) SEM and TEM images of carbonate globules and features resembling terrestrial microorganisms, terrestrial biogenic carbonate structures, or microfossils; (iv) magnetite and iron sulfide particles that could have resulted from oxidation and reduction reactions known to be important in terrestrial microbial systems; and (v) the presence of PAHs associated with surfaces rich in carbonate globules. None of these observations is in itself conclusive for the existence of past life. Although there are alternative explanations for each of these phenomena taken individually, when they are considered collectively, particularly in view of their spatial association, we conclude that they are evidence for primitive life on early Mars.

Recall the controversy you read about in Activity 2.2 and Section 2.2.1. Features in the Apex Chert were originally interpreted as fossils, but then were subsequently described as produced by the action of fluids travelling through the rocks. Those specimens have been examined by several different scientists over the years, using the most sophisticated analytical instruments available. Because the rocks come from a terrestrial locality, there is always the possibility of returning to the field and collecting additional samples. We know the geological context of the samples (i.e. where exactly the rocks came from), and still researchers argue whether the features are biological or not. Imagine, then, how much more difficult will be the discovery and certain identification of microscopic features in rocks on the Martian surface.

Question 3.4

What measurements might you make on Mars to see whether the rocks contain biological matter? (*Hint*: look back to Activity 2.2 and the measurements that Mojzsis and co-workers reported.)

Activity 3.4 Meteorites from Mars?

We expect this activity will take you approximately 30 minutes.

In order to try to show you the types of information that can be learnt from meteorites from Mars, you are now asked to read Article 8, which is an entry from the *Encyclopedia of Astronomy and Astrophysics*. You should access the article (entitled 'Meteorites from Mars') electronically through the Open University Library website. Follow the link given on the course website for Activity 3.4.

Article 8 was written by Monica Grady (now at the Open University and a member of the S104 course team, but at the time curator of the national meteorite collection at the Natural History Museum, London). The article gives some background to meteorites from Mars, and the reasons why scientists think that is where they come from.

After reading the article, carry out the tasks below which give you practice at extracting information. Have a quick look at the tasks now so that you can make notes as you read.

Task 1

Outline the argument for suggesting that some meteorites have come from Mars. (*About 100–150 words*)

Task 2

Outline three of the main things that we can learn about Mars from Martian meteorites. (*You should be able to do this in fewer than 100 words.*)

You should now read Article 8, consider your responses to the two tasks and then compare your answers with those in the comments on this activity at the end of this book.

Article 7, describing possible fossilised microorganisms in the Martian meteorite ALH 84001, is now several years old. So, it would be entirely reasonable to ask what developments have ensued in the intervening years. In brief, there has been an explosion of interest in Mars, life on Mars, Martian meteorites, and ALH 84001 in particular. There are many excellent resources (and some dubious ones!) on the Web that are dedicated to these issues – you can find some of the most informative by following the links given on the course website.

Although evidence has begun to pile up, interpretations and opinions have become increasingly polarised. Most scientists do not accept that the observations of features or chemical signals in ALH 84001 constitute evidence for past life on Mars. In contrast, a few die-hards believe the converse, i.e. that the evidence is entirely commensurate with past life. This is science in action. It seems clear to most people involved that the issue will not be adequately resolved until either samples are returned to Earth from Mars by space missions (perhaps by 2020), or the planet is explored properly by humans (perhaps 2030–2050).

Activity 3.5   What is the evidence for water on Mars?

We expect this activity will take you approximately 3 hours in total.

You have learnt about different ways in which we can find out about the planet Mars. You will now consider one specific aspect of a crucial requirement for life on Mars – evidence for the existence of water on Mars. You will undertake some investigations using web-based literature, and report results to your tutor group forum.

Now go to Activity 3.5 on the course website for instructions on this activity.

There are no comments on this activity.

3.2.3 Europa

You will now meet another body in the Solar System that is a candidate for life – one of the satellites of Jupiter, Europa. Europa is one of the brightest bodies in the Solar System. It 'shines', like all planetary bodies, by reflecting sunlight. It is bright because it reflects back a lot of sunlight, and it does this because its surface is ice, not rock. This satellite was studied in detail by the *Voyager 2* spacecraft, which showed this body of 1565 km radius to have an apparently smooth, featureless surface, described 'as smooth as a billiard ball' (Figure 3.6a). This indicates recent resurfacing. *Voyager 2* also showed that the majority of the surface of Europa was made of water ice. Images of Europa, taken by the *Galileo* spacecraft (Figure 3.14), show that the surface ice of the satellite is cracked, further demonstrating that there is continuing internal activity on the body. The conclusion is that the ice crust is being renewed from underneath by warm ice or, more importantly, liquid water. Indeed, there could be regions on Europa that are both warm enough, and sufficiently wet, to host life.

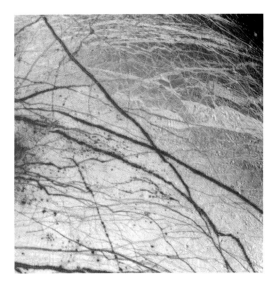

Figure 3.14   *Galileo* image of the cracked, icy surface of Europa. The area of view is 1260 km across. The image is coloured because it has been taken through filters to show that the surface is not completely homogeneous in composition. Some of the cracks are filled with slushy ice, and some are filled with mixtures of ice and dust.

It might be tempting to conclude from the smooth surface laced with cracks and the nearly pure water ice composition that Europa is a giant ball of ice. But measurements made by the *Galileo* spacecraft showed that the density of Europa is 3040 kg m^{-3}, which is much greater than that of water ice.

- ■ You have already encountered the density of liquid water, which is 1000 kg m^{-3} (at 0 °C and 10^5 Pa). How does the density of water as ice at 0 °C and 10^5 Pa compare with 1000 kg m^{-3}?

- ☐ The density of water ice is slightly *less* than 1000 kg m^{-3}, which is why ice floats on liquid water.

Ice would also float on a liquid water layer in the somewhat different temperatures and pressures of Europa. But on the basis of its density Europa cannot be composed largely of either pure ice or liquid water. To have a density as great as 3040 kg m^{-3}, Europa must be composed mainly of silicates. Currently, we do not know for certain what the interior of Europa is like. However, on the basis of the available evidence, there are two different models that describe the internal constitution of Europa, either of which could be correct. Europa might be rocky all the way through, topped by an ocean of liquid water capped by a thick layer of ice. Or it might have a metal core, above which is rock, followed by the ice-capped ocean. Magnetic and gravitational measurements cannot distinguish between these two models. Basically, we know the densities of metal, rock, ice and water, and can combine these figures in varying proportions to come up with a mean density that is close to that of Europa.

- ■ Why do you think that the presence of a liquid water ocean on Europa would be exciting for planetary scientists?

- ☐ Liquid water is one of the prerequisites for life. An ocean of liquid water on Europa, if confirmed, would open up the possibility that there is some form of life there.

The most vigorous debates concerning Europa are now directed towards the thickness of the icy crust and the depth of the ocean. This has consequences not only for the possibility of life on Europa, but also for whether we will ever be able to study it. Current estimates for the ice thickness are between 10–30 km above a 100 km deep ocean. Although engineers can conceive of instruments that may be able to penetrate a kilometre or two of ice, 30 km of ice covering a body far away from the Earth presents the most awesome of challenges. An analogous problem is currently concerning scientists and engineers who want to sample a freshwater lake (Lake Vostok) beneath 4 km of ice in Antarctica. Here, it is suspected that previously unknown life forms might exist, which have been cut off from the surface environment for perhaps millions of years. Should they exist, study of these entities will have a direct bearing on life in a wider Solar System context and will possibly be of relevance to some aspects of the environment on Europa. For more information on Europa, follow the links given on the course website.

Question 3.5

Sketch diagrams for each of the two models for the internal structure of Europa, that show the different layers and the relative thickness of each.

What prevents Europa's ocean from freezing? It is the pull of Europa's parent planet, the mighty Jupiter, which distorts the satellite as shown (greatly exaggerated) in Figure 3.15. As Europa orbits Jupiter its distance from Jupiter varies by small amounts because of its slightly elliptical orbit. As a consequence, the distortion also changes slightly, both in magnitude and in orientation, causing constant flexing of the satellite which, by friction, produces heat. This 'tidal heating' of Europa's interior supplements heat that comes from radioactive decay, maintaining the liquid ocean.

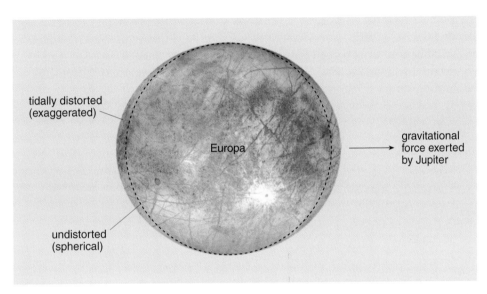

tidally distorted
(exaggerated)

Europa

gravitational
force exerted
by Jupiter

undistorted
(spherical)

Figure 3.15 Tidal distortion in the whole body of Europa (greatly exaggerated).

The combined effects of tidal and radiogenic heating in Europa will also create hot spots on the ocean floor. These may be analogous to environments on Earth where hydrothermal activity within the oceanic crust above magma chambers produces emergent hot springs (Book 2, Figure 7.4). Where these are released into Earth's oceans there exist oases capable of supporting life (even though the local temperatures may be in excess of 100 °C). Indeed, life on Earth might have started around such hydrothermal vent systems (Section 2.5.2). It seems possible that an environment similar to that in which thermophiles thrive on Earth could exist around deep oceanic vents on Europa.

In conclusion, Europa appears to have all the necessary requirements for life. It may have an ocean of liquid water, an abundance of biologically important elements (delivered by cometary and asteroidal bombardment) and energy sources in the form of sunlight and chemicals from submarine hot springs. Microorganisms could have evolved around hydrothermal vents at the interface between Europa's silicate core and the bottom sediment layers of the overlying ocean. As you can imagine, scientists would dearly love to send a spacecraft to the surface of Europa to search for signs of life. At the moment such missions are only at the conceptual stage.

3.3   Summary of Chapter 3

There are two questions pertinent to the issue of life within the Solar System beyond the Earth:

- Are there places where life may once have evolved but, for whatever reasons, did not survive?

- Are there examples of life elsewhere in the Solar System today?

The answer to these questions is that scientists simply do not know. Many planetary scientists would argue that on the balance of probabilities, the answer to both questions is 'no'.

'Life', within the context of Chapter 3, is confined to entities such as bacteria (prokaryotes) since it is known from our experience of life on Earth that bacteria are both widespread and have a primitive ancestry. If life got started anywhere beyond the Earth, then, irrespective of the extent to which it may have evolved, it should have at least passed through the single-celled stage. Thus, our search for life in the Solar System is essentially a search for environments capable of supporting single-celled organisms.

Most of the bodies of the Solar System (i.e. Mercury, Venus, Jupiter, Saturn, Neptune, Uranus, asteroids, and the Kuiper Belt Objects and comets) exhibit conditions that are, for one reason or another, considered unsuitable for life. In contrast, past or present environments on two bodies (Mars and Europa) are, at least in principle, capable of supporting life. A third body, Titan, could be experiencing the type of chemistry that led to life on Earth.

Conditions on Mars in the past appear to be compatible with what is required for the development of life. Results from spacecraft and Martian meteorites have not yet supplied unambiguous evidence for a Martian biosphere, and so the question of life on Mars remains, so far, unresolved.

Europa, a large satellite of Jupiter, is a body that has a generally smooth, icy crust with no craters, which suggests relatively recent internal activity. A possible structure of Europa has a deep layer of liquid water beneath a surface layer of ice, the liquid water overlying a large silicate-rich core, which might still be warm enough to generate hot spots. Conditions at the core–ocean interface may be analogous to those around hydrothermal vents on Earth. If so, it is possible that Europa could support, or even is supporting, life.

Chapter 4
Life beyond the Solar System

In this chapter you will explore the possibility of life beyond the Solar System. Because the most likely place to find life is on the surface of a planet in orbit around a star (or on the surface of a satellite in orbit around such a planet), the first step in the search for life is to find planets orbiting other stars – extrasolar planets, or exoplanets. You will look at how this has been attempted, and with what success. You will then consider how such extrasolar planets can be investigated for signs of life.

4.1   The search for extrasolar planets

In Book 2, Section 13.1.1 you learned that there are about 10^{11} stars in the Galaxy, and that they are arranged in space in the manner of Figure 4.1.

■   Where is the Sun in Figure 4.1?

☐   The Sun is in the Galactic disc, about half way from the Galactic centre to the edge of the disc (marked as 'S' in both parts of Figure 4.1).

Because the Sun is in the disc, it is in a region of the Galaxy that is relatively well populated with stars. Figure 4.2 shows, on a larger scale, our immediate stellar neighbourhood, where the spacings between the stars are on average a few parsecs (pc; where 1 pc = 3.1×10^{13} km). There are approximately 2000 stars within 30 pc of the Sun, and about 50 000 within 100 pc.

■   What is 100 pc in kilometres?

☐   1 pc = 3.1×10^{13} km

   So 100 pc = $100 \times 3.1 \times 10^{13}$ km = 3.1×10^{15} km.

Although 100 pc is a long way by terrestrial standards, it is a short distance by cosmic standards, and modern techniques of planet detection could certainly hope to find any planets around stars within 100 pc of the Sun, perhaps further. Therefore there are already many tens of thousands of stars that are targets for investigation.

When you think about detecting planets, a method that might spring to mind is direct imaging, in which a planet is seen as a point of light separate from its star. There is, however, a problem with this method that can be illustrated if you consider a pinhead held a few centimetres from a powerful streetlight at night. From a range of several kilometres, the light reflected by the pinhead would be drowned out by the powerful light received directly from the streetlight. The situation is similar for stars and planets. For example, if we were looking at the Solar System from a distance of only 10 pc, the solar radiation reflected even by the giant planet Jupiter would be entirely drowned out by the direct solar radiation received by our detectors. So it is very difficult to detect extrasolar planets directly. There have been reports of the direct detection of a planet

Figure 4.1   Two schematic views of the Galaxy: (a) face view and (b) edge view. The disc is about 40 000 parsecs (pc) across and about 600 pc thick. The position of the Sun is labelled 'S' in the figures. 1 pc = 3.1×10^{13} km (Book 7 Section 8.1).

(a)

(b)

orbiting the star GQ Lupi (about 450 light-years, or 135 pc, from the Sun), but it is not yet certain if the object is indeed a planet or merely a very small companion star in a binary (two-star) system.

In Sections 4.1.2 to 4.1.5, you will consider four different techniques for detecting extrasolar planets by indirect methods. Before doing so, however, in order to appreciate these different methods, you will revisit some principles of gravity and motion from Book 2 Chapter 14.

4.1.1   The effect of a planet on stellar motion

The planets in our Solar System are held in their orbits by the gravitational force that the Sun exerts on them. This is a universal force. Therefore the planets also exert a gravitational force on the Sun, and the magnitude of the gravitational force that the Sun exerts on a planet is the same as the magnitude of the gravitational force that the planet exerts on the Sun. For example, if the

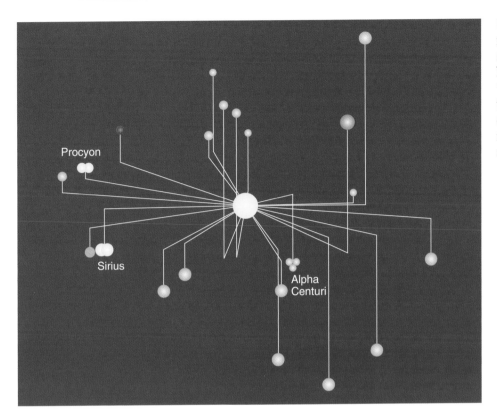

Figure 4.2 The stellar neighbourhood of the Sun showing the 25 nearest stars. Note, in this case, the term 'star' includes systems of two or three stars in orbits around each other. The sizes of the spheres representing the stars increases as the luminosity increases.

gravitational force that the Sun exerts on Jupiter has a magnitude F_J, then the magnitude of the gravitational force that Jupiter exerts on the Sun is also F_J. Thus the Sun must be accelerated by Jupiter. The outcome is that as Jupiter orbits the Sun, the Sun goes around an orbit of its own. However, the acceleration of the Sun is small.

From Newton's second law of motion (Book 2 Section 14.2), an expression for the magnitude of the acceleration a_S of the Sun can be obtained in terms of Jupiter's mass, m_J, and the Sun's mass, m_S. Newton's second law of motion states that, for any mass m:

$$F = ma \qquad (4.1)$$

Applying this to the case in hand:

$$F_J = m_J a_J \quad \text{and also} \quad F_J = m_S a_S$$

Thus $m_S a_S = m_J a_J$ and so, dividing both sides by m_S:

$$a_S = \frac{m_J a_J}{m_S} \qquad (4.2)$$

The mass of the Sun is about 1000 times greater than the mass of Jupiter, and this fact can be used, in combination with the above equations, to determine the relative sizes of the orbits of the Sun and Jupiter.

Take Equation 4.2 and divide both sides by a_J:

$$\frac{a_S}{a_J} = \frac{m_J}{m_S} \qquad (4.3)$$

As m_S is about $1000 \times m_J$, then this shows that the acceleration of the Sun, a_S, must be about 1000 times less than the acceleration of Jupiter, a_J.

To use this expression to determine the relative sizes of the orbits of the Sun and Jupiter, it helps to imagine a planetary system consisting of a star with a mass m_{star}, and a single planet with a mass m_{planet} that is as much as 0.2 times (or 20% of) the stellar mass. Also suppose that the planetary orbit is circular. In this case the orbits of the star and planet are as shown in Figure 4.3. The planet moves in a circular orbit around a point on a line between the two bodies, and the star goes around the same point also in a circular orbit. Note that the orbital periods of both bodies around this point are the same, and that this is also the orbital period of the planet as seen from the star. The ratio of the orbital radii, $\dfrac{r_{star}}{r_{planet}}$, is the same as the ratio of the accelerations:

$$\frac{r_{star}}{r_{planet}} = \frac{a_{star}}{a_{planet}} \tag{4.4}$$

■ For the system in Figure 4.3, what is the ratio $\dfrac{r_{star}}{r_{planet}}$?

☐ By applying Equations 4.3 and 4.4 to this system:

$$\frac{r_{star}}{r_{planet}} = \frac{a_{star}}{a_{planet}} = \frac{m_{planet}}{m_{star}} = 0.2$$

Therefore, $\dfrac{r_{star}}{r_{planet}}$ should be 0.2.

The point around which both bodies move is called the **centre of mass** of the system. You can get a feel for the centre of mass by imagining (or building!) a model of the system in Figure 4.3, with two balls connected by a thin lightweight

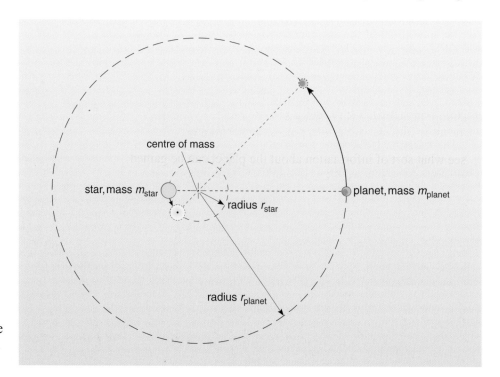

Figure 4.3   A star with a planet with a mass that is 20% of the star's mass – a greatly exaggerated planetary mass. The orbits are circular and presented face-on to the reader.

rod. The centre of mass is the point on the rod where the balls and stick balance, and do not tip over one way or the other. Predictably, the balance point is nearer the more massive ball. You can also simulate the orbital motion. If you were to push a pin at right angles through the rod at the point of balance, and rotate the system around the pin, then this is how the star and planet orbit the centre of mass.

You have just established a general result, which can be expressed compactly as an equation:

$$\frac{r_{\text{star}}}{r_{\text{planet}}} = \frac{m_{\text{planet}}}{m_{\text{star}}} \tag{4.5}$$

Thus, for the Sun, if Jupiter were the only planet in the Solar System, the radius of the Sun's orbit would be about 1000 times less than the 7.8×10^8 km radius of Jupiter's orbit. The presence of the other planets complicates the picture, but because Jupiter is the most massive planet by some margin, the outcome is not greatly changed. The average radius of the Sun's orbit is thus only about 10^6 km, about the same as the Sun's radius. Nevertheless, observers with our technology on planets around nearby stars could detect the orbital motion of the Sun and hence deduce the existence of the more massive planets in the Solar System.

Stars are sources of copious radiation, and this enables us to measure their positions and motions very accurately. In practice, there are two main techniques for detecting stellar orbital motion, and these will be described now.

4.1.2 The astrometric technique: the measurement of stellar positions

Figure 4.3 shows a stellar orbit presented face-on to you. Suppose that the orbital period is 5 years, and that the centre of mass in this system is stationary with respect to stars that are so distant that they constitute an apparently fixed background. Therefore, over a period of 5 years, the star will move around a circular orbit with respect to the stellar background, as in Figure 4.4. By measuring the position of the star for several years, its orbital motion can be detected, and the existence of the planet inferred. This is the basis of the **astrometric technique**: the detection of planets by measuring the position of a star at various points in the star's orbit.

To see what sort of information about the planet can be gained from astrometry, it is useful to rearrange Equation 4.5 so that the mass m_{planet} is the subject.

One way to perform this rearrangement is to swap the equation left to right, and multiply both sides by m_{star}. The result is:

$$m_{\text{planet}} = m_{\text{star}} \left(\frac{r_{\text{star}}}{r_{\text{planet}}} \right) \tag{4.6}$$

To obtain m_{planet} the three quantities on the right-hand side of Equation 4.6 need to be known. These can be determined by observing the star, but the details need not concern you here.

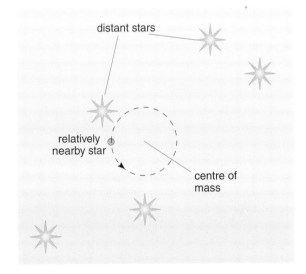

Figure 4.4   A nearby star moving in a circular orbit with respect to an apparently fixed background of more distant stars.

The important point is that with the three quantities on the right-hand side of Equation 4.6 known, m_{planet} can be calculated. The astrometric technique thus gives the mass of a planet and the radius of its orbit. Its orbital period is the same as that of the star (Section 4.1.1), so that value is also found.

Note that to establish the existence of a planet the star must be observed for an appreciable fraction of the orbital period. In the Solar System, the orbital period of Jupiter is nearly 12 years, so it can take some time to build up data on stellar positions that would reveal any planetary system.

Question 4.1

A planet is in orbit around a star that has a mass about 0.8 times that of the Sun. It has been established that, as measured from the centre of mass of the system, the radius of the star's orbit is 2×10^6 km, and the radius of the planet's orbit is 3×10^8 km.

(a) Given that the mass of the Sun is 1.9891×10^{30} kg, calculate the mass of the planet.

(b) Given that the mass of the Earth is 5.974×10^{24} kg, calculate by what factor the mass of this planet exceeds the mass of the Earth.

4.1.3 The radial velocity technique: the measurement of stellar velocities

Suppose that the system in Figure 4.3 were presented edgewise to you, so that your viewpoint was along the page, rather than perpendicular to it. In this case, instead of a circular path in the sky, the star would appear to move from side to side across the sky. The astrometric technique can still be used to reveal the masses and orbits of the planets. However, a second technique is now available. This is possible because the star is moving towards us during half its orbit, and away from us during the other half, i.e. it has a variable speed in the radial direction, a variable 'radial velocity'. This motion can be detected because of the Doppler effect (Book 7 Section 8.2).

■ What is the Doppler effect?

☐ In the Doppler effect, there is a change in the wavelength of the radiation received from a source, when the source is in motion with respect to the observer.

When the star is moving towards us, its spectral lines are shifted to shorter wavelengths (blue-shifted), and when it is moving away from us its spectral lines are shifted to longer wavelengths (red-shifted). By detecting these shifts we can infer the presence of the planet. Figure 4.5 shows the spectral shifts at various points in the edgewise orbit.

The oscillating Doppler shift arising from the orbital motion of the star will be superimposed on the Doppler shift arising from the steady motion of the whole system towards or away from us. However, the two contributions are readily distinguished, the oscillation appearing as a periodic variation in the

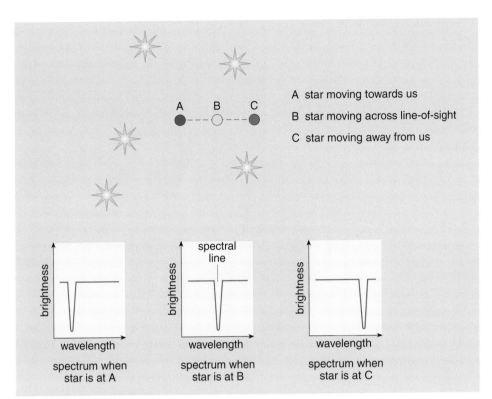

A star moving towards us

B star moving across line-of-sight

C star moving away from us

Figure 4.5   An edgewise view of the orbital motion of a star with respect to an apparently fixed background of more distant stars, plus the corresponding Doppler effect on the wavelength of an absorption line in the star's spectrum.

steady shift. The amplitude of this oscillation is called the Doppler amplitude, and (for a given mass of star) it is proportional to the mass of the planet.

This **radial velocity technique** is capable of detecting planets at greater ranges than the astrometric technique. Provided that the star is bright enough to have readily visible spectral lines, then it does not matter how far away it is – there is no diminution with distance in the size of the wavelength changes. By contrast, in the astrometric technique, the greater the range from which the orbit in Figure 4.4 is viewed, the smaller the star's orbit will appear on the sky.

There is, however, a disadvantage with the radial velocity technique. For a given system, if the orbit is presented face-on, as in Figure 4.4, then the star does not move towards and away from us in its orbital motion, and so there are no oscillating Doppler shifts – the Doppler amplitude is zero. At the other extreme, the case in Figure 4.5, the variation in radial velocity is a maximum, and so we get the maximum Doppler amplitude for this particular system. If the system were presented at some intermediate angle then we would get an intermediate Doppler amplitude. This introduces an ambiguity. Imagine that you observe a system and measure a certain Doppler amplitude. You do not know the angle at which you are seeing the system. If you assume it is near to edge-on then you would deduce a certain mass m_{edge} for the planet. If, in fact, the system is not near edge-on then, to produce the same Doppler amplitude, the planet must have a mass greater than m_{edge}. This is because only a proportion of the star's motion is now along the radial direction. The radial velocity technique does not reveal the angle of view, and so the planetary mass obtained from this technique is the *minimum* value m_{edge}, i.e. it could be greater. It is the *actual* mass only if the system is presented edge-on.

A rough estimate of the angle of view can be obtained from the way that the rotation of the star modifies its spectral lines. The important point is that we can do rather better in many cases than merely obtaining a lower limit to the planet's mass.

Activity 4.1   Changing radial velocity of a star

We expect this activity will take you approximately 30 minutes.

Table 4.1 lists the radial speed v_r (the magnitude of the radial velocity) of a star, as calculated from Doppler shifts, at 02.00 hours every five days.

Table 4.1 The radial speed of a particular star.

time/day	0	5	10	15	20	25	30	35
v_r/km s^{-1}	24.059	24.034	24.023	24.013	24.017	24.042	24.068	24.088
time/day	40	45	50	55	60	65	70	75
v_r/km s^{-1}	24.086	24.086	24.059	24.044	24.022	24.014	24.019	24.044

(a) Plot these data (i.e. radial speed against time) on Figure 4.6.

(b) State (in one sentence) why your plot indicates that there might be a planet in orbit around this star.

(c) If indeed there is a planet, what is its orbital period? Estimate the uncertainty in the period.

Now look at the comments on this activity at the end of this book.

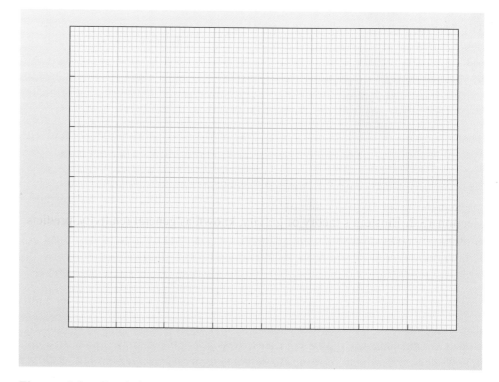

Figure 4.6   Graph for Activity 4.1.

4.1.4 The planetary transit technique

Another technique for the indirect detection of planets is to measure the effect a planet has on the light curve (i.e. how its brightness varies with time) of its star as the planet passes in front of the star.

■ If your view is exactly edge-on, or very nearly so, what event, once per orbit, could reveal the existence of the planet?

☐ The planet will pass between you and the star, resulting in a small decrease in the brightness of the star.

This is the **planetary transit** or occultation technique – the planet occults ('hides') part of the star (Figure 4.7). It requires a very good chance alignment of the planet's orbital plane with our line of sight, and so this method can reveal only a very small fraction of planetary systems. However, if a very large number of stars is observed, then the probability of seeing a drop in the light curve of a star increases. This is the idea behind the SuperWASP project (Wide Angle Search for Planets), which comprises two robotic telescopes. One of the telescopes is in the Northern Hemisphere, on the island of La Palma in the Canaries, whilst the second is in the Southern Hemisphere at the site of the South African Astronomical Observatory near Sutherland, South Africa. Each telescope comprises an array of eight wide-angle cameras with sensitive imaging detectors, which scan the sky automatically each night. The project only started observing in mid-2004, and announced the first discovery of two Jupiter-sized planets, WASP1b and WASP2b, in September 2006. Astronomers from the Open University are part of the consortium of eight academic institutions that devised and run the SuperWASP programme.

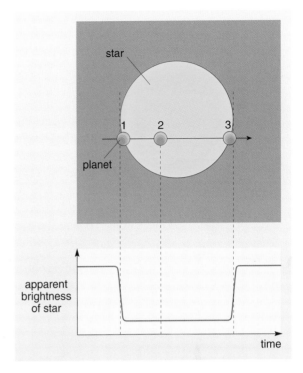

Figure 4.7 The transit of a planet across the face of a star results in a decrease in light from the star. The light curve associated with the transit is shown.

4.1.5 Gravitational microlensing

The fourth and final method of indirect extrasolar planet detection to be considered is that of gravitational microlensing. As you saw in Book 7 Section 13.2, Einstein's theory of gravity, known as general relativity, predicts that massive objects distort space. One effect of this is that the path of light can be 'bent' when it travels close to massive objects, and this is seen as gravitational lensing of distant objects by nearer, intervening galaxy clusters. Such gravitational macrolensing can lead to multiple or distorted images of the background object. On a smaller scale, and somewhat nearer to home, gravitational **microlensing** is the name given to the bending of light by individual stars and planets. The stars in our galaxy are all in constant motion, mostly orbiting around the centre of the Galaxy every few hundred million years, but with a range of speeds and directions. If, as a result of this motion, one star passes *directly* in front of another, as seen from our line-of-sight, then the nearer star will cause gravitational microlensing of the more distant star. The result is an amplification or sudden brightening of the light from the background star. The foreground and background star cannot be seen as two separate points of light – they are too closely aligned for that – but the combined light signal brightens, then fades in a characteristic manner (as shown in Figure 4.8a) over a period of typically a week. More than 1000 microlensing events like this have been observed over the past few years. Just occasionally, however, something else is seen. If the nearer (lensing) star has one or more planets in orbit around it, then it may happen that the planet too lenses the background star. The result is an additional brightening superimposed on the main lensing event (as shown in Figure 4.8b). The advantages of the technique are that very distant planetary systems can be detected and also that very low-mass planets can be seen, but the disadvantage is that the events do not repeat, so there is no possibility of studying the orbits of the exoplanets so detected.

There is currently a large survey underway: the Optical Gravitational Lensing Experiment, or OGLE, which is using a 1.3 m telescope in Chile to survey many thousands of stars to look for the effects of gravitational lensing. At the time of writing (late 2007), this campaign had detected several planets, the smallest of which was only about 5.5 times as massive as the Earth, and which now rejoices in the name OGLE-2005-BLG-390Lb.

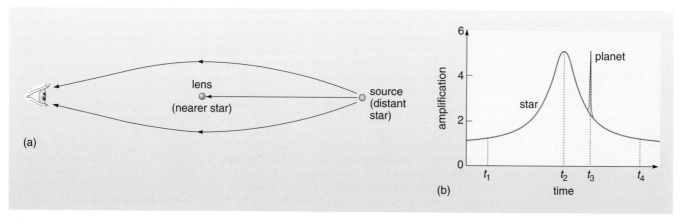

Figure 4.8   Gravitational microlensing of a distant star by a nearer star; (a) a line-drawing to show the path of light from a distant star and how it is deflected by a second star closer to the observer; (b) the light curve associated with the microlensing event, and how it is modified if a planet is in orbit around the distant star.

Activity 4.2   The first cool rocky/icy exoplanet

We expect this activity will take you approximately 15 minutes.

In the previous few sections, you have learnt about the different techniques by which extrasolar planets can be observed. Figure 4.9 is a plot that shows the mass and orbital radius of the planets observed to date by these different techniques. The planet masses are given relative to the mass of the Earth, m_E.

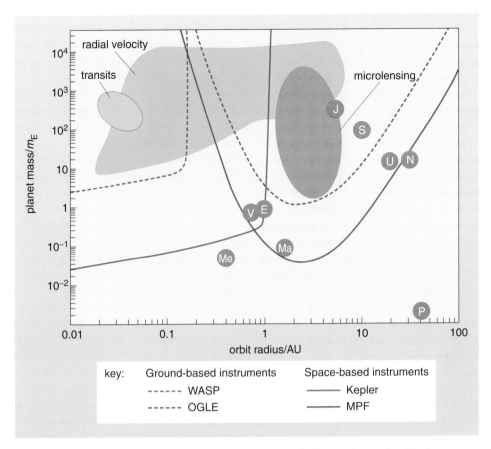

Figure 4.9   A plot to show the detection limits of planet size and orbit for different observation techniques. Radial velocity observations fall in the orange area, those from transit techniques in the blue area and gravitational microlensing in the red area. The solid and dashed lines define the regions on the figure within which planets are detectable by the specified instruments. Kepler is a NASA space telescope, to be launched 2009. Abbreviations: OGLE – Optical Gravitational Lensing Experiment (uses a ground-based telescope in Chile, described in Section 4.1.5); MPF – Microlensing Planet Finder (a proposed NASA space telescope under consideration); WASP – Wide Angle Search for Planets (uses two robotic ground-based telescopes, described in Section 4.1.4). The grey dots show where our Solar System objects would lie on this diagram. The plot is adapted from Figure 2 in Dominik et al. (2006).

Task 1

Why are the space-based instruments (solid) lines lower than the ground-based instruments (dashed) lines?

Task 2

(a) Which of the different techniques can detect the planet furthest away from its star? (b) Why is this? (c) Which technique will detect the smallest planet?

Now look at the comments on this activity at the end of this book.

4.1.6 The easiest types of planet to detect

In Sections 4.1.2 to 4.1.5, you learnt of four different techniques that could be used to detect extrasolar planets indirectly, through observing the motion of stars or their light curves.

■   What sort of planet, in terms of its mass and its orbit, would be the easiest to detect with indirect techniques?

☐   For all the indirect techniques, the greater the mass of the planet, and the closer its orbit is to the star, the greater the effect on its star, and so the easier it is to detect.

Consider the two systems in Figure 4.10, and suppose that they are at the same distance from the Earth, and that the mass of the star, and the separation between the planet and the star, are the same in both cases. The systems differ in that in (a) the planet is 0.2 times the mass of the star, whereas in (b) it is 0.1 times the stellar mass.

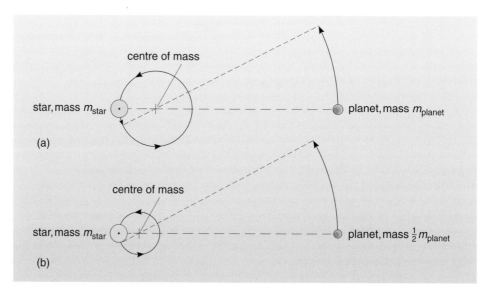

Figure 4.10   Two planetary systems, which differ only in that the mass of the planet in system (b) is half that in system (a).

■   What is the ratio $\dfrac{r_{\text{star}}}{r_{\text{planet}}}$ of the orbital radii in each system?

☐   From Equation 4.5, the ratio is 0.2 in system (a), in which the planet is 0.2 times the mass of the star, and 0.1 in system (b).

Because the star–planet separation is the same in both cases, you can see from Figure 4.10 that the larger stellar orbit is in the system with the larger mass planet. The larger the stellar orbit, the easier it is to measure with the astrometric technique. This is also the case for the radial velocity technique. This is because the orbital periods in Figure 4.10 are determined by the total mass of the system. Therefore, because the star accounts for nearly all of this mass in each system, the times it takes the stars to get around their orbits are not very different. This means that the star with the larger orbit has to move faster. Consequently, the greater the mass of the planet, the greater the variation in Doppler shift of the stellar spectral lines.

Consider now the two systems in Figure 4.11, in which the masses of the stars are again the same, but now so too are the masses of the planets. The systems differ in the distance between the star and its planet. The centre of mass is again located in accord with Equation 4.5. Therefore, the greater the star–planet distance, the greater the radius of the star's orbit, and the easier it is to measure with the astrometric technique.

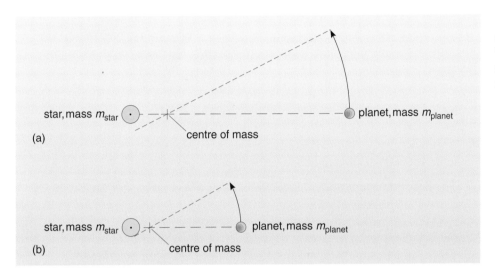

Figure 4.11 Two planetary systems, which differ only in that the distance between the star and the planet in system (a) is twice that in system (b).

With regard to the radial velocity technique, the outcome is less obvious. On the one hand, the smaller the star–planet distance, the smaller the radius r_{star} of the star's orbit, but on the other hand it turns out that the star's orbital period P is also smaller. The speed of the star in its orbit is proportional to $\frac{r_{star}}{P}$, but with r_{star} and P both reduced, it is not obvious which effect 'wins'. It turns out that P is more reduced than r_{star}, and so the orbital speed is greater for smaller star–planet distances. Consequently, the larger variations in Doppler shift of the stellar spectral lines occur with the smaller orbits. Therefore, the smaller the planetary orbit, the easier it is to detect the planet with the radial velocity technique. The reduced orbital period of the star also carries the additional advantage that a complete orbit is observed in a shorter time.

Question 4.2

Imagine two as yet undiscovered planetary systems, in each of which a planet with the same mass as Jupiter is in orbit around a solar-mass star. Table 4.2 lists other properties of these systems. For each system discuss whether the astrometric technique or the radial velocity technique is the more likely to detect the system, or whether there is little to choose between the two techniques.

Table 4.2 Some properties of imaginary planetary systems in which a Jupiter-mass planet is in orbit around a solar-mass star.

System	Distance of system/pc	Star–planet distance / Jupiter–Sun distance[*]	Angle of view
A	10	10	nearly face-on
B	1000	0.1	nearly edge-on

[*] The Jupiter–Sun distance is 7.8×10^8 km, or 2.5×10^{-5} pc.

4.1.7 Results from planet detection techniques

The discussion turns now to the results from the indirect techniques. Up to 1995, this would have been a very short account indeed! Then the situation changed dramatically. In 1995, 51 Pegasi was identified as the first Sun-type star to have a planet in orbit around it. A giant planet eight times closer to 51 Pegasi than Mercury is to our Sun was observed using the radial velocity technique. Since then, many more planets have been recognised. You can access an up-to-date catalogue by following the link given on the course website. At the time of writing (late 2007), 276 planets had been confirmed, contained within 238 planetary systems.

Many of the planets, like the one orbiting 51 Pegasi, have become known as **hot Jupiters** – they are giant planets orbiting very close in to the central star.

■ Assuming that there are Earth-mass planets in some of the systems, why has none yet been discovered?

☐ The lower the mass of the planet, the less its effect on its star, so low-mass planets are less easy to find.

Earth-mass planets are presently beyond detection by the radial velocity technique, and also by the astrometric technique. They are potentially detectable by the transit technique, but only if the star is very small and if the orbit is edge-on.

Question 4.3

Why is it unsurprising that a system like 51 Pegasi was the first extrasolar system to be discovered, and that it was discovered with the radial velocity technique?

Figure 4.12a shows the number of planets with masses m_{edge} lying within various mass ranges, i.e. the mass distribution of over 250 planets. The mass unit is the mass m_J of Jupiter, 318 times the mass of the Earth and the most massive planet in the Solar System. The minimum mass m_{edge} is used for each exoplanet because these planets were all discovered by the radial velocity technique, and only in a few cases are there reliable estimates of the angle of view. You can see that the smaller the mass range, the greater the number of planets in it, with the greatest number of exoplanets in the range $0–1m_J$.

The question arises of whether all the true masses are considerably greater than m_J, as would be the case if all the orbits were nearer face-on than edge-on. This is extremely unlikely – if the orientation of the orbits is random, then it can be shown that the vast majority of planets will have masses less than a factor of two greater than m_{edge}. So, the masses of these planets are predominantly less than ten times the mass of Jupiter.

But are they also like Jupiter in composition, dominated by the light elements hydrogen and helium, and therefore unsuitable for life (Section 3.1.2)? This question can be answered if the planets' radii are known. An Earth-like planet will have a composition dominated by the heavy elements that constitute rocks, and will be smaller than a hydrogen–helium planet of the same mass. The radius

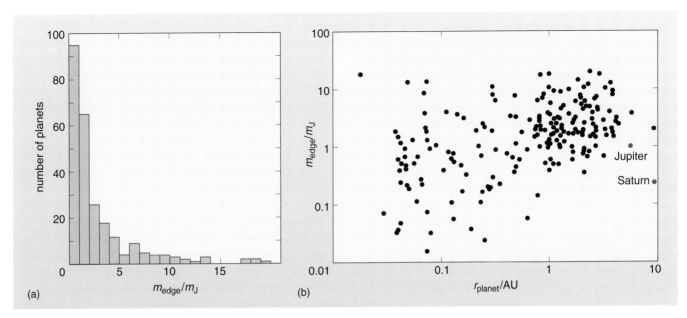

Figure 4.12   (a) The mass distribution of approximately 250 planets discovered by the radial velocity technique. (b) The planet's mean orbital radius, r_{planet}, in astronomical units, AU (1 AU is the average distance between the Earth and the Sun – Section 3.1). (Note the mean orbital radius is often written as 'semimajor axis', a, in scientific literature.)

of a planet can be obtained by the transit technique, and many of the exoplanetary systems have been scrutinised in this way. So far, fewer than 10% of the planets discovered by the radial velocity technique have also been shown to occult their stars. Results for the planet orbiting the star HD209458 show that the planet is a bit bigger than Jupiter with an actual mass (we are seeing the orbit edge-on) of $0.69m_J$. This certainly rules out a rocky-iron composition and shows that this planet is much more like Jupiter than Earth in composition. There are in any case great difficulties in understanding how any circumstellar disc (Section 4.1.8) could have contained enough heavy elements to make hundreds of Earth masses of rock and iron. There is a consensus that practically all of the planets so far discovered are more like the giant planets in our Solar System than they are like the Earth.

Though the exoplanetary systems contain 'Jupiters', nearly all of them have orbits very different from that of Jupiter, which orbits the Sun in an almost circular orbit.

In contrast, many of the exoplanets have very elliptical orbits, particularly those not so close to their star. Equally remarkable, most of the exoplanets have far smaller orbits than that of Jupiter, which has a mean orbital radius of 5.2 AU (Figure 4.12b). In comparing orbits, note that the scales in Figure 4.12b have unequal increments, as you can see from the values on the axes. These are logarithmic scales, which you have met before.

■   Estimate the mean orbital radius of the smallest orbit in Figure 4.12b.

☐   The smallest orbit has an a value of about 0.03 AU.

These innermost giants are therefore about 30 times closer to the star than the Earth, at 1 AU, is to the Sun. Any 'Jupiter' closer to its star than 1–2 AU could not have formed there – the circumstellar disc would have been too hot and too sparse. Computer models, that model how rotating and turbulent discs of dust and gas behave, show that giant planets must have formed farther out and then interacted with the remnants of the circumstellar disc so that they migrated inwards.

The first spectra from an exoplanet were reported in 2007, taken by the Spitzer Space Telescope. This is a telescope orbiting the Earth which measures the infrared (IR) spectra of objects. It has not yet detected any new planets, but it has taken the IR spectra of several planets that had previously been discovered by transiting techniques, including that of planet HD209458b. The spectrum of star HD209458 (mentioned above) was recorded whilst the planet was behind the star, and then again as the planet passed in front of the star. When the first spectrum was subtracted from the second, the 'leftover' light was interpreted as being from planet HD209458b. Again, this is an indirect, rather than a direct detection, and did not produce an image of the planet, just a possible IR spectrum. As discussed above, HD209458b was the first exoplanet to be discovered by the transit method, and was inferred to have a mass of 0.69 times that of Jupiter, and a slightly larger radius. These measurements would imply that the planet is a gas giant. However, the spectral data did not record any methane or water vapour in the planet's atmosphere, although astronomers did observe a signal interpreted to be from very hot silicate particles. It is thought that these particles might form high-level clouds of dust that are obscuring other signals.

Is the Solar System unusual? Probably not. Giant planets close to the star are the easiest to detect by the radial velocity technique (Section 4.1.3). Therefore there could be many systems not that different from the Solar System awaiting discovery. Moreover, among many of the systems already discovered, it is possible that Earth-like planets could survive at just the right distance from the star for them to be habitable. The range of appropriate distances is called the **habitable zone** of the star, and it is generally taken to be the region within a planetary system where conditions are sufficiently suitable and stable for life to arise. The habitable zone is sometimes called the 'Goldilocks Zone' because conditions are not too hot, and not too cold – they are just right for life. The habitable zone is often taken to be the zone where, given sufficient atmospheric pressure, liquid water would be stable on the surface of a planetary body. The Sun's habitable zone is centred on 1 AU (the Earth's distance from the Sun).

Question 4.4

(a) What consequences might the inwards migration of a giant planet have for the formation or survival of Earth-like planets in the habitable zone of a star?

(b) Once inwards migration has ceased, what is required for the subsequent formation of Earth-like planets in the habitable zone?

So far, a few thousand nearby stars have been investigated, with a concentration in the searches on solar-type stars. A few per cent are known to have planets, and this number will surely grow as the more difficult discoveries of giants in large orbits are made. That planetary systems might indeed be common, and therefore potential habitats too, is indicated by the presence of circumstellar discs around many stars.

4.1.8 Circumstellar discs

It is thought that the planets in the Solar System originated from a disc of gas and dust around the young Sun (Book 2 Section 11.4). If this is right, and if planetary systems are common, then many young stars today should have such discs – **circumstellar discs**. The first was discovered in 1983, around the star Beta Pictoris. An image of this disc is shown in Figure 4.13. It is presented almost edge-on, and is visible through the light from its star that it scatters. Detailed studies have revealed that the disc has a hollow centre, like a doughnut. Distortion of the disc at the edge of the hollow indicates the presence of planets within the hollow.

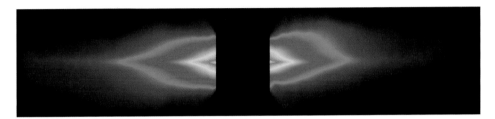

Figure 4.13   The dust disc around the star Beta Pictoris, seen at visible wavelengths via the light it scatters from its star. The disc is presented nearly edge-on. Beta Pictoris is obscured to enable the disc to be seen.

By the time the 51 Pegasi system was discovered in 1995, many more circumstellar discs around young stars were known, and Figure 4.14 shows two of them. This image was made by the Hubble Space Telescope at visible

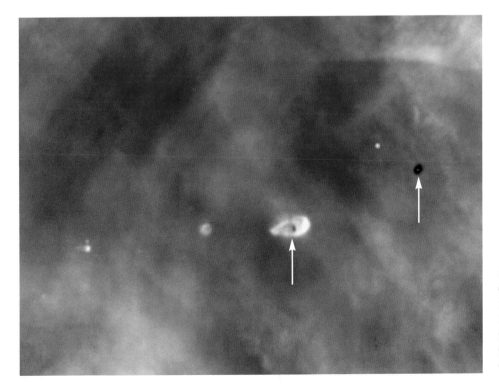

Figure 4.14   Two circumstellar discs (arrowed) in the Orion Nebula, about 500 pc from Earth, imaged by the Hubble Space Telescope; the dust is seen at visible wavelengths.

wavelengths. It reveals what seem to be discs of dust and gas surrounding two newly formed stars. These fuzzy blobs could be infant solar systems in the making. Discs can also be imaged at infrared wavelengths, via the infrared radiation that the dust particles emit.

■ What would have to happen to the temperature of the dust for it to emit sufficient visible radiation to be detected?

☐ The dust temperature would have to increase (Book 3 Section 8.5).

At even longer wavelengths – radio wavelengths – we can detect spectral lines emitted by the molecules of the gas in the discs, and more discs have been discovered this way. It is clear that the majority of young stars have discs of dust and gas around them. Thus, with an abundance of discs from which it is believed planetary systems form, it is likely that planetary systems themselves are common.

With all the indirect evidence indicating that planetary systems are not rare, perhaps common, astronomers are being inspired to great efforts to obtain images of extrasolar planets. Though such imaging is not yet feasible, what are the prospects for the near future?

4.1.9 Imaging of planets

A major obstacle to obtaining images of extrasolar planets has already been noted.

■ What is it?

☐ The light reflected by the planet is feeble compared with the light of its star, and the two bodies appear to be so close together from our distant vantage point that the starlight overwhelms the light from the planet.

To see how best to overcome this obstacle you need to know something of how telescopes work.

Large astronomical telescopes are **reflecting telescopes** – they collect light by means of a large dish-shaped mirror, as in Figure 4.15. The mirror forms an

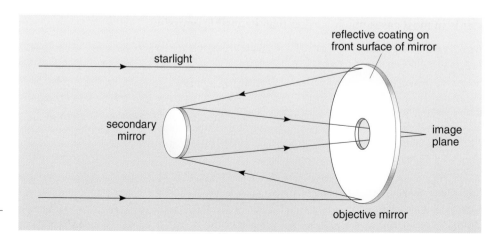

Figure 4.15 A telescope that uses a mirror to form an image – a reflecting telescope.

image by focusing light via the secondary mirror onto the image plane, where a detector can be placed to record the image. The mirror acts like the big lens at the front of a pair of binoculars, or like a camera lens. For large telescopes, mirrors are preferred to lenses because they are cheaper and give better quality images. You can demonstrate that a dish-shaped mirror forms an image if you have a mirror that magnifies you when you look into it (such as some shaving mirrors or some make-up mirrors). Direct the mirror at a window a few metres away, and place a piece of paper in front of the mirror, as in Figure 4.16. Move the paper forwards and backwards and you will find a position where you obtain an image of the window.

For reasons that are beyond the scope of this book, the amount of detail in the image is limited by the size of the mirror. All we need to note here is that the larger the mirror (or lens) the finer the detail in the image. In other words, there is a degree of blurring in the image, and the larger the mirror, the smaller the degree of blurring. A star is so far away that the telescope 'should' produce an image that is little more than a point. In reality it produces a much larger image, a blurred disc. The blurred disc is brightest in its centre and gradually fades towards the edges, as in Figure 4.17a. The top part of the figure is an impression of what the image might look like, and the graph beneath it is the variation in brightness along a line across the centre of the image. Any planet will also be imaged as a blurred disc of the same diameter as the image of the star, though far fainter. Thus, as Figure 4.17a shows, the image of the star overwhelms the image of the planet. However, if the mirror were sufficiently large, the images of star and planet would disentangle, as in Figure 4.17b, and the planet would be seen.

Note that in Figure 4.17 the difference in brightness between the star and the planet has been greatly underplayed. In reality the planet is far, far fainter, particularly at visible wavelengths where we have light emitted by the star and starlight reflected by the planet. At infrared wavelengths things are not quite as bad, because we now have longwave infrared emission from the planet, and the longwave infrared emission from the star is in most cases much weaker than its visible emission.

The largest telescopes today that work at visible or infrared wavelengths have huge mirrors about 10 m in diameter. However, to obtain images of planets around nearby stars we need telescopes that are much larger even than this. Fortunately the crucial dimension is the distance of one edge of the mirror from another; there does not have to be mirror filling the whole area! Thus the single huge mirror in Figure 4.18a produces images with detail no finer than that from the array of smaller mirrors in Figure 4.18b. The downside is that the actual collecting area of the array is less, so longer exposures have to be used to collect enough light get a suitably bright image. It also takes many exposures with the mirrors in different orientations to build up the detail. In spite of this, and though highly sophisticated techniques are required to combine the images from

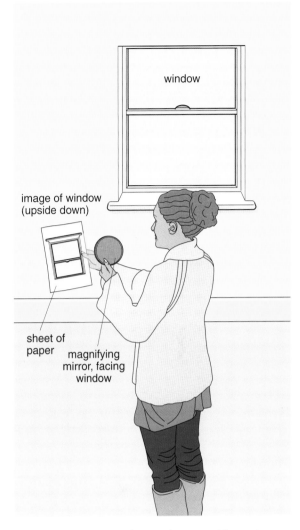

Figure 4.16 Forming an image with a mirror that magnifies.

window

image of window (upside down)

sheet of paper

magnifying mirror, facing window

Figure 4.17   Illustrative light distributions across the images of a star and its planet produced by (a) a large telescope, and (b) a very large telescope.

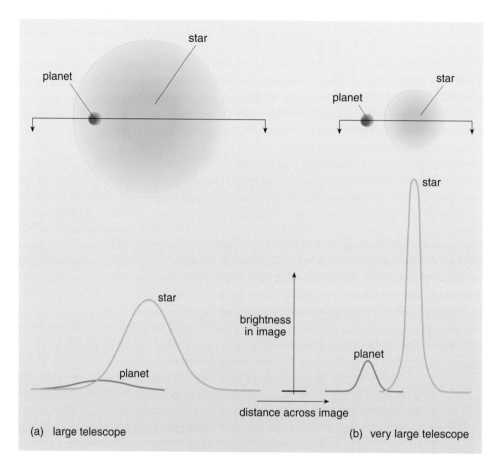

Figure 4.18   (a) A single mirror 100 m across. (b) An array of smaller mirrors that produces the same fine detail as the single mirror in (a). Note that the 10 m diameter mirrors in (b) are as large as the largest single mirrors today that work at visible or infrared wavelengths.

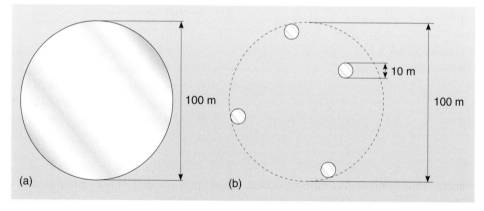

the separate mirrors in an array, a telescope constructed from an array of small mirrors is much cheaper than a single mirror many metres in diameter. The array approach is called **interferometry**, a term you will meet in any further reading about this subject. Figure 4.19 shows the four largest telescopes in one array, the Very Large Telescope. The latest news from these telescopes can be found by following the link on the course website.

Some large mirrors today are not single, but made up of segments fitted together. Examples are the two Keck telescopes on Mauna Kea in Hawaii. Each of these is 10 m in diameter but made up of 36 hexagonal segments 1.8 m across. The segments are kept in accurate positions by a sophisticated dynamic adjustment system at the back of each segment. By using many segments rather than a single mirror there is the cost advantage of mass production, and this makes it feasible to contemplate what are called Extremely Large Telescopes, or ELTs. One design under study is by the European Southern Observatory, and is called OWL, which can either be regarded as being named after the eye of an owl, or standing for OverWhelmingly Large telescope. OWL would have a segmented mirror 100 m in diameter so could obtain images of planets around nearby stars. For the latest news on OWL, or the E-ELT (for European Extremely Large Telescope) as it is now called, follow the link on the course website.

Highly sophisticated techniques are also used to overcome another problem – the image-blurring effect of the Earth's atmosphere. The atmosphere is not a perfectly homogeneous optical layer but varies in its optical properties as a result of small variations in density from place to place. The pattern of variation is constantly changing because of the winds, and the result is a blur that wobbles about, rather like the view of the bottom of a busy swimming pool from a vantage point above the surface. Atmospheric blurring prevents telescopes from giving the detail we expect from a mirror of given diameter. There are two ways of overcoming this problem. One is a technique called **adaptive optics**, in which the atmospheric motions are monitored, and appropriate compensating adjustments are made many thousands of times per second to the optical layout of the telescope.

Figure 4.19   The four large cylindrical buildings that house the four 8-m-diameter telescopes of the Very Large Telescope (VLT) at the European Southern Observatory site on Cerro Paranal in Chile. In addition to these four large telescopes there are also a few smaller ones. Overall, the array will give detail corresponding to a single mirror about 200 m across. Completion of the array is expected in 2010.

■   What might be the other way of overcoming blurring due to the atmosphere?

☐   The other solution is to place telescopes in space, above the atmosphere.

4.1.10 Space-based exoplanet searches

A space telescope is a better technical solution than adaptive optics, though for a telescope of a given size it is very much more expensive.

There are several telescopes already in space that are searching for extrasolar planets. Two systems, the Hubble Space Telescope (working in the visible part of the spectrum) and the Spitzer Space Telescope (infrared) are not dedicated to the search, but have discovered extrasolar planets as part of their continuing observation programmes.

The joint France-ESA mission, *CoROT* (launched in December 2006) and NASA's *Kepler* mission (October 2008) are both dedicated to searching for extrasolar planets by transiting techniques. Each instrument is designed to make continuous observations of areas of the sky, monitoring about 100 000 stars over the duration of the missions. The first results from *CoROT* were announced in May 2007.

Looking further to the future, both ESA and NASA are planning to launch space missions to detect extrasolar planets. ESA is considering a mission called *Plato*

(PLAnetary Transits and Oscillations of stars) that will detect and characterise transiting planets (including rocky planets) as well as measuring the seismic oscillations of their parent stars. It may be launched around 2020. Further into the future (2025 or beyond), ESA has a mission under study called *Darwin*, an array of small telescopes that will perform interferometry. NASA has also been planning a mission called *Terrestrial Planet Finder*, which also has no definite launch date. The latest news on these projects can be found by following the link on the course website.

The current position is that the direct imaging of planets is not quite within our capabilities. However, astronomers know how to do it, and there is a good prospect that within the next two decades we shall have the first images of planets around other stars. As soon as we have such images, we shall be able to search the planets for biospheres. This search is described in Section 4.2.

Question 4.5

(a) Consider the following two proposals, for telescopes to work at visible wavelengths:

System 1: A single mirror, 20 m diameter, at ground level, and employing adaptive optics.

System 2: An array of four mirrors in space, each mirror being 1 m in diameter, and separated from its neighbours by 100 m.

  (i) Why would each system be very expensive? (ii) Which system would be less affected by the Earth's atmosphere? (iii) Which system would give sharper images?

(b) What would be the advantage of working at longwave infrared wavelengths when trying to observe extrasolar planets?

4.2 The detection of life

As mentioned above, within a few decades, it is likely that the first image of an extrasolar planet will have been obtained. This will probably be no more than a fuzzy dot, at the limit of our instrumental capabilities. How shall we be able to tell if there is life on the planet? Travel to the planet will probably be out of the question, but there are a number of remote investigations that could be made.

4.2.1 Atmospheric spectroscopy

One of the most important investigations would be to establish whether any atmosphere existed and, if so, to establish its composition. This could be achieved by passing the radiation from the planet through a spectrometer and examining the spectral lines (Book 3 Section 8.4). The presence of certain absorption or emission lines would reveal that an atmosphere existed, and the wavelengths of the lines would indicate its composition. As mentioned in Section 4.1.7, there have been observations by the Spitzer Space Telescope that have already given us the composition of the surface layers of one extrasolar gas giant. This particular planet seemed to be hot and dry, and circled by clouds of incandescently hot silicate grains.

If water vapour were detected in the atmosphere of a rocky exoplanet, and if further measurements showed that the surface temperatures and pressures fell within the range at which water exists as a liquid, then we could conclude that liquid water is present over some or all of the surface.

■ Why would this be an exciting discovery in relation to extraterrestrial life?

☐ One of the necessary conditions for life as we know it, is liquid water (Sections 2.1.2, 2.4 and 3.1).

With the scientific belief that, given the right conditions for life, it is almost certain that life will emerge, we would feel optimistic that on that fuzzy dot a biosphere was present.

But could we be *certain* that life had actually emerged?

■ Using your knowledge of Book 1 and Book 6, and Chapter 2 of this book, describe a global effect of the Earth's biosphere on the Earth's atmosphere.

☐ The Earth's biosphere influences the composition of the atmosphere. Oxygen in the atmosphere is almost entirely a product of photosynthesis, and is sustained by photosynthesis. Without its biosphere, the Earth would soon lose the oxygen from its atmosphere.

If we were to detect evidence of oxygen in abundance, then it would be *fairly likely* that there was an active biosphere; we know of no better way than photosynthesis of sustaining a substantial quantity of a highly reactive gas like oxygen in the atmosphere. Oxygen would be easier to detect as ozone (O_3) rather than the form we breathe (O_2), but this would make no difference – detectable quantities of ozone require much greater quantities of O_2. If there were oxygen *and* evidence that liquid water was present, then this would make it *very likely* that there was an active biosphere.

Another important discovery would be evidence of methane (Activity 3.1). A trace of methane and an abundance of oxygen would be a very strong indication of the existence of a biosphere. On Earth, the trace of methane is sustained largely through bacterial metabolism. Without such biospheric processes, the methane level would be far, far lower, because it is so readily oxidised by the oxygen.

It would thus be possible to detect a living biosphere. But the converse is not true. For example, if there were no oxygen we could not conclude that there was no biosphere.

■ Has the Earth always had an oxygen-rich atmosphere?

☐ No. For most of Earth history the oxygen level was low (Chapter 2 and Book 6 Section 3.1).

The low level of atmospheric oxygen lasted for the first 2200 Ma or so of terrestrial history. Throughout that enormous span of time, the rate of oxygen production was insufficient to overcome the loss of oxygen through the oxidation of rocks, volcanic gases and dead biomass. Only from about 2400 Ma ago did the oxygen level in the atmosphere begin to rise. Suppose though, that the evidence for a biosphere on an extrasolar planet was very strong. It would be tantalising to come to this conclusion, but to be unable to find out much about it. Yet that is exactly the position we are likely to be in, unless, somehow, life can tell us about itself. One way in which this could happen is described next.

4.2.2 The search for extraterrestrial intelligence

Assume that there is an extrasolar planet on which an intelligent species has emerged, and that this species had developed and is using technology to attempt interstellar communication. In this case, if we detected and interpreted their signals, then the whole process of searching for planets and then investigating them would be short-circuited. We would at once know that there was life out there, and that it had become intelligent.

The **search for extraterrestrial intelligence (SETI)** is, by its nature, a very speculative project. However, in 1961, very early on in the development of the SETI programme, Frank Drake, an astronomer working at the National Radio Astronomy Laboratory in Greenbank, Virginia in the US, put forward an argument that provided a framework in which the probability of finding an extraterrestrial intelligence could be considered. This led to what is known as the Drake equation, which is an expression that attempts to quantify the number (N) of extraterrestrial civilisations in our galaxy that could be detected by their electromagnetic emissions. N is dependent on a number of factors. One form of the Drake equation is:

$$N = R \times f_g \times f_p \times n_e \times f_l \times f_i \times f_c \times L \tag{4.7}$$

N = the number of extraterrestrial civilisations in the Milky Way galaxy whose electromagnetic emissions are detectable

R = rate of formation of stars

f_g = fraction of stars suitable for supporting life

f_p = fraction of those stars with planetary systems

n_e = number of planets, per planetary system, with an environment suitable for life

f_l = fraction of suitable planets on which life actually appears

f_i = fraction of life-bearing planets on which intelligent life emerges

f_c = fraction of civilisations that develop a technology that releases detectable signs of their existence into space

L = length of time such civilisations release detectable signals into space.

You are not expected to memorise this equation, but to understand that it is a guideline for research and discussion.

The Drake equation was very conjectural when it was first presented – but almost 50 years later, we are in a position where we can realistically start to estimate the number of Earth-like planets in the Galaxy. And in a few more years, we should be able to know something about the type of atmospheres that envelope these planets. So we are starting to populate the expression with realistic values. A discussion of the Drake equation is described in Activity 4.3.

Activity 4.3   W(h)ither the Drake equation?

We expect this activity will take you approximately 15 minutes.

In Article 9, called 'W(h)ither the Drake equation?', Mark Burchell (2006) takes the latest estimates of the different parameters of the Drake equation and discusses how they have changed since Frank Drake first put forward the relationship. Mark Burchell is a Professor at the University of Kent at Canterbury, specialising in impact physics. He has carried out high-velocity impacts of bacteria-impregnated rock into rocky and icy surfaces to assess the probability of microorganisms surviving impact following interplanetary or interstellar transit. Article 9 was published in the *International Journal of Astrobiology*, a journal that was only established in 2001, to publish the growing number of papers that were being written on different aspects of the developing discipline of astrobiology.

You should access the article electronically through the Open University Library website. Follow the link given on the course website for Activity 4.3. After reading the article, carry out the tasks below which give you practice at extracting information. Have a quick look at the tasks now so that you can make notes as you read.

Task 1

There are eight terms on the right-hand side of the Drake equation. Which terms are we most likely to derive values for based on observations or scientific models?

Task 2

Using Equation 4.7, calculate a value for N, if $R = 10 \text{ y}^{-1}$, all the fraction terms are 0.5, n_e is 2, and L is 10 000 years.

You should now read Article 9, consider your responses to the two tasks and then compare your answers with those in the comments on this activity at the end of this book.

Discussion of SETI is not just the stuff of science fiction. We have the capability of signalling across the Galaxy, and yet our technological civilisation is very young. How much more capable might be older civilisations? Since 1959, groups of scientists have been searching the skies for signals, mainly by using radiotelescopes to search for radio signals, but now also by searching for visible light and infrared signals. This is an important aspect of SETI. So far (and in spite of the ever popular but misguided cover-up theories), no signals of unambiguously intelligent origin have been detected. But is this search a worthwhile activity, or a waste of time and money? What are the chances that there are other technological civilisations in the Universe with which we could communicate?

You will doubtless have come to your own conclusion about the likelihood of detecting extraterrestrial intelligence. It is difficult to predict the probability of success, given all the unknowns, though the lack of success so far indicates that civilisations attempting interstellar communication at radio wavelengths are at best rare in our region of the Galaxy. For the nearest stars we can also conclude that there are probably no civilisations that, like ours, leak radio communications into space without any deliberate attempt at interstellar communication. These leakages would probably be far more difficult to detect than the signals from deliberate attempts, which is why, so far, we can only exclude such civilisations for the nearest stars.

Surely the issue of extraterrestrial intelligence is such a huge and fascinating one that it is worthwhile to devote a small resource to searching? Fortunately, with recent developments in instrumentation and software it is possible to do a lot of searching on a shoestring. Success is not assured, but the scientific reward for success would be huge.

On the question of life in general, rather than intelligence in particular, we already know that planetary systems are not rare, and few scientists disagree with the view that there must be life (not necessarily intelligent life) elsewhere in the Galaxy, perhaps widespread. If so, then among the few thousand stars that we can see with the unaided eye, there might well be several orbited by a planet on which life has emerged. It is all the more exciting that we are within decades of having the capability of placing the issue beyond reasonable doubt.

4.3   Summary of Chapter 4

To discover life beyond the Solar System, the first step is to discover planets, and the second step is to investigate whether any of them support life. The discovery of planets would be bypassed through the discovery of signals from extraterrestrial intelligence, though there is considerable disagreement among scientists about the likelihood that technological civilisations exist beyond the Earth.

Over 250 extrasolar planetary systems had been discovered in the neighbourhood of the Solar System by late 2007, and the number is growing monthly. These have been discovered indirectly, mainly by the radial velocity technique, although transit and gravitational microlensing search programmes are starting to report discoveries. Most of the planets are gas giants, but a few rocky planets with masses less than 10 times the size of the Earth have been identified. Some of the planets are in orbits that challenge our understanding of how planetary systems form. It is inferred that planetary systems with Earth-sized planets are not rare.

Evidence that planetary systems might be common is provided by the large proportion of young stars that are encircled by discs of gas and dust – discs that in many cases will surely be the birthplace of a planetary system, and in other cases provide evidence that a planetary system has already formed.

Developments in instrumentation and techniques over the next few decades will make it possible to obtain images of planets. Once such images are obtained it will be possible to examine the radiation from planetary atmospheres for evidence of life. Suitable conditions for the emergence and sustenance of life would be indicated by the presence of water vapour in the atmosphere and by surface temperatures and pressures in the ranges that permit water to be liquid at the surface. If liquid water were present, then given our belief that, if the conditions for life are right, life will emerge, we would be optimistic that a biosphere was in place, particularly if oxygen was also present, though an absence of oxygen would not rule out life.

A very strong indication of an active biosphere would be the discovery of appreciable quantities of oxygen along with traces of methane, though the absence of these substances would not mean that a biosphere was also absent.

Chapter 5
Summary of Book 8

This book began with two big questions:

- How did life begin on Earth?
- Is there life elsewhere in the Universe?

These questions have not been fully answered here. Nor would complete answers be found in any other text. We know little for certain about the origin of life on Earth, and though we have plausible theories about many of the stages, some other stages are very obscure. The transition from molecules to cells is perhaps the greatest mystery, especially the nature of the genetic material that carried information to organise the system. Suggesting that RNA was used before DNA is only a partial solution, because RNA is still a very complex molecule. Perhaps simpler molecules carried information before RNA. There is little prospect for much progress in the near future, perhaps not for decades, unless we discover unequivocal evidence of life or fossils beyond the Earth; such discoveries would provide valuable extra data.

The question of whether there is life elsewhere in the Universe could in principle be resolved tomorrow if intelligent signals were to be detected (or if extraterrestrials were to pay us a visit!). Within the Solar System, forthcoming space missions may soon show whether there is life today on Mars, or whether there are fossils from a long-gone Martian biosphere.

Beyond the Solar System, the observational evidence that planetary systems are not rare, perhaps common, plus the scientific belief that life will emerge whenever the conditions are right, means that even among the few thousand stars visible to the unaided eye, there might be a few planetary companions with life. The next few decades should yield a crop of Earth-sized extrasolar planets, and the subsequent investigations of their atmospheres might reveal incontrovertible evidence for life. Whether intelligent species have emerged in any of those biospheres will be far less certain.

Throughout this book, you have been reading scientific articles and noting information from them. You have also practised planning an account (Activity 2.6). In the following activity, you will write an account that uses some of the articles that you have read, referencing them appropriately. This is a crucial skill for a scientist, as 'doing science' is only of use to others if you can communicate your work appropriately.

Activity 5.1   Writing an extended account

We expect this activity will take you approximately 3 hours.

In this activity you will use the plan that you prepared in Activity 2.6 to produce an extended account. Having already prepared a plan (and in the light of the comments on Activity 2.6) you should find it relatively straight forward to produce the complete account.

Write a 500–600 word account that answers the following question:

What are the various means by which life might have originated on the Earth?

Your account should include references where appropriate, with the full references listed at the end.

Ensure you complete your account before you look at the comments on this activity at the end of this book.

Chapter 6
Science explored

You have now reached the final section of the final book of this course, and if you look back over the eight books you will appreciate that a vast area of science has been covered. You started in Book 1 with global warming – a topic that is of great interest and concern, and is affecting each one of us – and you have ended by exploring topics that are at the forefront of current research, where scientists are still asking fundamental questions about the origin of the Universe and the origin of life. Along the way you will have developed your understanding of the way that the natural world works and of the ways in which scientists find out about how it works.

Exploring science is an unusual course in many respects, and one of these is the way that it brings together the different disciplines of science. From the start of the course we were keen to raise your awareness of the role of science in the world around us and in everyday life. Earth science, physics, chemistry and biology have all played their part in our understanding of global warming, and equally they all have a part to play in trying to answer the questions covered in this book about life in the Universe.

We have also been keen to avoid delineating the different science disciplines too clearly. In real life, science is a continuum, and is not rigidly compartmentalised. The boundaries between chemistry and biology are very blurred when it comes to topics such as enzyme chemistry and understanding the action of drugs at the cellular level. Similarly the boundaries between Earth science and physics become very blurred when we are considering radioactive decay processes in the Earth, radiometric dating and the behaviour of seismic waves. These fuzzy boundaries are also apparent in the transitions between some of the books in this course. Biological evolution led us naturally into the study of the fossil record and the history of the Earth, which in turn led to the study of the history of the Universe from the time of the big bang. All of these aspects of evolution and history are reflected in the final book, and the quest to discover life elsewhere in the Universe.

We hope that studying *Exploring science* has whetted your appetite to learn more about science. We also hope that you are better equipped with a sound science base to contribute to informed debate about topical issues. One of the characteristics of scientists is that they ask (and answer) questions, and generally the more answers that they come up with, the more questions they are spurred to ask. One of the important ideas that we have tried to convey is that science is not a cut-and-dried subject. It is dynamic, alive and developing. At various stages in human history people have pronounced that all the important science had been discovered, but this has never proved to be the case. There are still important questions that scientists are investigating. How will the Earth's climate react to increasing CO_2 levels? Can we design drugs to combat AIDS? How can we explain the periodic mass extinctions of life? Is there life elsewhere in the Universe?

But stepping back from the questions that research scientists are attempting to answer, we hope that studying the course has set up all kinds of questions in your mind – that it has left you wanting to find out more about particular areas.

There will undoubtedly have been some parts of the course that you found more exciting and interesting than others. These are likely to be the parts about which you have lots of questions that you want to find answers to, and you can discover some of these answers by studying more advanced science courses in the appropriate area.

And, finally, as well as meeting a wide variety of science, you have also developed and improved many skills. These skills will be of use to you in future courses and in other areas of your life. To identify some of the skills developed, we suggest that you try the final activity of the course.

Activity 6.1   Reflecting on your study of S104 and thinking about future study

We expect that this activity will take you approximately 20 minutes but you may wish to spend longer, depending on how far you want to explore particular aspects.

As you have studied S104, you will have developed a tremendous number of skills. These have undoubtedly proved useful to you during the course, but we hope that they will prove (or already have proved) useful in other parts of your life. Learning outcomes for the course include cognitive, key and practical skills and we have teased out what these involve at various points in the course. In this book you will have made particular use of your communication skills, applying knowledge and understanding gathered across the whole course.

Task 1

To conclude your study of S104, note down three or four skills that you have developed while studying this course which you have found particularly useful, and record an example of an occasion when you used each skill. You may find it helpful to think of the things that you can do now that you would not have been able to do (or not do so well) when you started the course. You may also wish to add some comments about why you have found the skill useful and/or advice to yourself about its further use or development. If you have continued to record where course learning outcomes have been taught, developed and assessed on the grids provided for Books 1 and 2, you will have a rich resource of information to refer back to that will refresh your memory for this task.

Task 2

Now think about the knowledge and understanding you have developed through the course. What areas have you enjoyed or find particularly interesting? What did you find difficult or challenging? What do you want to find out more about? We would like you to think about any plans you have for study in the future, if you've not already done this. Note down now where you wish to go after S104 and your personal action plan to achieve this.

As this activity is personal to you, there are no comments on this activity.

As you have worked through S104, we have encouraged you to take notes, refer back and revise earlier material. Book 8 has drawn heavily on your previous study. Now is the time to consolidate your knowledge and understanding in revising to prepare for the final course assessment.

Answers to questions

Further comments on the answers are given in square brackets [...].

Question 2.1

From the composition of Murchison we can assume that the primitive Earth would have been bombarded with significant amounts of organic compounds, including amino acids, and water.

Question 3.1

Comets are presumed to be unchanged since the Solar System formed, and so by studying dust from a comet, we are looking at the original material that made the planets.

Question 3.2

A good way of summarising the internal constitution of the giant planets is to draw a sketch, equivalent to the appropriate half of Figure 11.9 of Book 2, as in Figure 3.16.

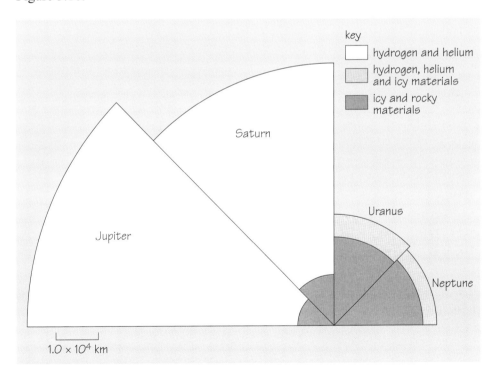

Figure 3.16 The internal constitution of the giant planets. Note that the boundaries are probably less well defined than shown here.

Question 3.3

There is effectively a surface upon which life could exist – dust particles. There is a reasonable temperature (about 0 °C) at some parts of the atmosphere. We are not sure about nutrients, but comets could replenish the atmosphere with vital components. And there is water, which could condense on the particles. So, at face value it would appear that life is at least possible.

Question 3.4

First of all you would need to determine whether or not there was any carbon present in the rocks. If carbon were present, then you would need to find out whether it was organic or inorganic. To find out if any organic carbon present was biological in origin, you would measure its carbon isotopic composition.

Question 3.5

Two models for the internal structure of Europa are given in Figure 3.17.

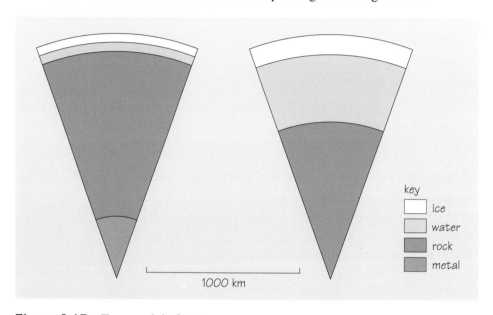

key
☐ ice
☐ water
☐ rock
☐ metal

1000 km

Figure 3.17   Two models for Europa.

Question 4.1

(a) From Equation 4.6, the mass of the planet is:

$$m_{planet} = (0.8 \times 1.9891 \times 10^{30} \text{ kg}) \times \left(\frac{2 \times 10^6 \text{ km}}{3 \times 10^8 \text{ km}} \right)$$

$$= 1 \times 10^{28} \text{ kg}$$

to one significant figure (as the orbital radii are only known to one significant figure).

(b) The mass of this planet divided by the mass of the Earth is:

$$\frac{1 \times 10^{28} \text{ kg}}{5.974 \times 10^{24} \text{ kg}} = 1674$$

which is 2000 (to one significant figure). Thus the planet's mass is about 2000 times the mass of the Earth. [This is about six times the mass of Jupiter.]

Question 4.2

System A

The nearly face-on view would make the Doppler variations very small. Moreover, the planet is not particularly close to the star and so, even edge-on, the Doppler variations would not be particularly large. By contrast, the system is only 10 pc away, and the star–planet distance is large, and so there would be a readily detected stellar orbit on the sky. Thus the astrometric technique is the more likely to detect the planet's presence. [The orbital period, however, is *very* long, so it would take many years to build up sufficient positional data.]

System B

The radial velocity technique is the more likely detection method here. The nearly edge-on view maximises the variation in the Doppler shifts, and these would be large because of the small star–planet separation. This same small separation makes the stellar orbit small, and the system is a long way off, and so the astrometric technique is disadvantaged. [If the system were very nearly edge-on, then there might be occultations of the star by the planet.]

Question 4.3

The planet around 51 Pegasi is massive and in a small orbit. Therefore it gives rise to Doppler shifts that vary rapidly over a wide range of values. It is not a good candidate for the astrometric technique because the stellar orbit is small.

Question 4.4

(a) A giant planet migrating into or across the habitable zone would be likely either to remove any Earth-like planets that had already formed, or to scatter the smaller components from which such a planet might have been forming. [In fact the latter is more likely, because of the relatively long time it takes for the final stages of building an Earth-like planet. It is also sufficient for the giant to approach the habitable zone – it need not enter it because, as it migrates, the changing gravitational forces it exerts on material in the habitable zone will be sufficient disturbance.]

(b) To form an Earth-like planet there must be sufficient rocky-iron material in the habitable zone. This must be able to come together to build an Earth mass, and therefore the giant must be in an orbit not too close to the habitable zone. [It is plausible that enough material will be left swirling about, and provided that the giant is not near the habitable zone it is plausible that an Earth-mass planet or two could form.]

Question 4.5

(a) (i) System 1 is expensive because it is a single mirror of enormous size, and System 2 is expensive because it is in space.

(ii) Although System 1 uses adaptive optics, this is not quite as good as getting above the Earth's atmosphere, as System 2 does, so System 2 is less affected by the Earth's atmosphere.

(iii) System 2 will give sharper images than System 1 because it has a larger overall size, though it will take longer to acquire the images.

(b) The advantage of working well into the infrared is that the ratio of brightness of the planet to the brightness of the star is greater than at visible wavelengths.

Comments on activities

Activity 2.1

The completed Figure 2.1 is given in Figure 2.9. It shows the following nine dates and events: (1) 4360 Ma (the age of the oldest minerals); (2) 4100 Ma (the first presence of water on Earth); (3) 4030 Ma (the age of the oldest rocks, the Acasta gneiss); (4) 3850 Ma (the presence of chemical trace fossils in the Akilia rocks); (5) 3800 Ma (the date of the late heavy bombardment); (6) 3500 Ma (the presence of biological tracers in the Apex Chert); (7) 3400 Ma (the presence of bacteria, shown by stromatolites and the occurrence of hopanes in rocks); (8) 2700 Ma (the presence of eukaryotes, shown by the occurrence of steranes in rocks); (9) 2400 Ma (time when oxygen began to accumulate in the Earth's atmosphere).

Events numbered 1, 3, 7 and 8 should be marked in style 1 (red on Figure 2.9), as they are ages obtained by direct measurement. Events numbered 2, 4, 5, 6 and 9 should be marked in style 2 (blue on Figure 2.9), as they are ages inferred from other evidence.

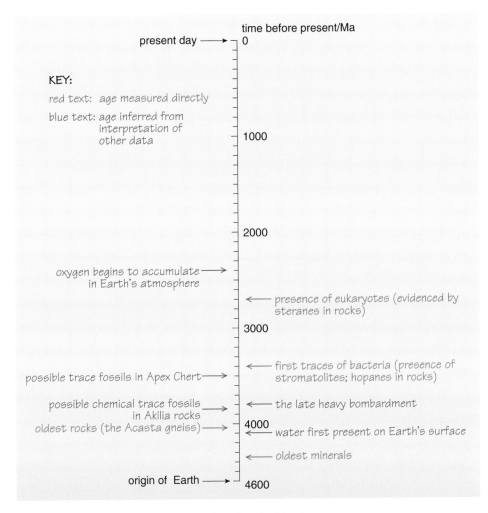

Figure 2.9 The completed timeline for the Earth.

Activity 2.2

Task 1

The piece of geological evidence is the age of zircon crystals dated by U–Pb dating.

Task 2

Isotope ratio data (the ratio of the two carbon isotopes ^{13}C and ^{12}C) in the Isua rocks from Greenland provides evidence for the presence of carbon derived from living systems. The graphite could have been produced by thermal dissociation (i.e. breakdown on heating) at 450 °C of iron-rich carbonates to produce iron oxide, carbon dioxide and elemental carbon (graphite). [There are further comments about this data in the comments in the text that follows this activity.]

Activity 2.3

Task 1

The first landmark is the delivery of cosmic building blocks to Earth by comets and asteroids. The second landmark is LUCA, the last universal common ancestor, which might be a population of organisms rather than a single organism.

Activity 2.4

Task 1

Immediately after the Moon formed, the Earth's atmosphere would have been a mixture of vaporised rock and gas. As this cooled and silicates rained out, the atmosphere became mainly CO_2, CO, H_2O and H_2, along with minor amounts of N_2 and noble gases. The water would be present as steam.

Task 2

After the impact that formed the Moon, the Earth was so hot (>2000 K) that it was surrounded by clouds of rock vapour. The temperature of the Earth's surface gradually cooled, and the vapour condensed, forming an ocean of molten silicate (magma ocean) at <2000 K. The magma ocean lasted for about two million years before it solidified, giving the Earth a rocky crust. The temperature then cooled from about 500 K to 200 K.

Activity 2.5

Task 1

Ferris and colleagues took some clay minerals and sprinkled them into a solution of activated RNA nucleotides. The clay minerals acted both as a surface and a catalyst for polymerisation of the nucleotides into chains up to 10 nucleotides long (after a few hours) and up to 50 nucleotides long after a few weeks.

Task 2

Orgel and colleagues showed that by repeatedly adding (or feeding) low concentrations of monomers (or building blocks) to clay minerals, longer chains (polymers) were formed than in the absence of clay. Nucleotide monomers formed nucleotide chains and amino acids formed amino acid chains (peptides).

Thus solid mineral surfaces catalyse the formation of polymers that are precursors of important macromolecules in cells. The significance of these results is that they suggest how one problem in chemical evolution leading to the origin of life (hydrolysis of long chains) might have been avoided. (*90 words*) [This is developed in the text following the activity.]

Activity 2.6

Compare the plan that you produced with the plan below, which was produced by a member of the course team. She has written the introduction and conclusion in full, but the plan for the main body of the account is in note form. Your plan is likely to be a lot less detailed and probably includes various abbreviations – it only needs to be intelligible to you, whereas the plan here needs to be intelligible to a large number of other people.

Introduction

From a scientific viewpoint, there are only two ways in which life might have originated on Earth: by chemical evolution of life from simple chemicals, or by immigration of some form of life from an extraterrestrial source. Both of these mechanisms are described and compared in this account.

Chemical evolution

Paragraph 1: Chemical evolution – simple organic molecules evolved into more complex molecules from which, eventually, living cells were organised (Section 2.4); e.g. amino acids to proteins, sugars to complex carbohydrates, nucleotides to nucleic acids.

Great uncertainty about how process happened, many different hypotheses. Hypotheses based either on simulation experiments, e.g. Miller's and Ferris' experiments or similar (see Articles 2 and 4, Section 2.4.1) or guessing state of the Earth when life is thought to have evolved and then predicting what sorts of chemical reactions could have occurred, e.g. Article 3.

Paragraph 2: Origin of simple organic molecules on early Earth.

* early hypothesis of Miller (generation in strongly reducing atmosphere by action of UV radiation) now regarded as unlikely.

Other hypotheses:

* origin in shallow pools or at ocean surface (Section 2.4.1)
* origin on pyrite particles in the atmosphere (Section 2.4.1)
* simple organic molecules reached Earth from space via dust particles, comets or meteorites.

Paragraph 3: Origin of more complex organic molecules.

* presumably in the same place(s) that simple molecules originated
* problem of hydrolysis and need to maintain high concentrations of reactants (Section 2.4.1) led to suggestion that solid surfaces were important (Article 4).

Paragraph 4: Final stage: macromolecules to living cells. First cells probably autotrophic (Section 2.4.2). Must have had surrounding membrane – could have been important for conversion of external energy source into 'useful' energy (e.g. ATP) by proton pumping. Also needed way to store and replicate information – possibly RNA, but simpler system could have operated in first cells, e.g. self-replicating molecules organised on a mineral template (Section 2.4.3).

Extraterrestrial origin

Paragraph 5: Life, in some heat-resistant form (e.g. spores or single cells protected by layer of carbon – Section 2.5.3) reached Earth on dust particles or interior of meteorites. Presumption that life arose by chemical evolution on another planet?

Comparison of hypotheses and their relative likelihood

Paragraph 6: Both hypotheses assume life originated by chemical evolution:

- chemical evolution hypothesis suggests it occurred on Earth
- extraterrestrial hypothesis suggests it was on another planet.

Possible argument against chemical evolution on Earth – insufficient time between the Earth cooling down and earliest known life (Section 2.4)?

Argument against ET origin – organisms unlikely to survive in space and during descent through Earth's atmosphere. No firm evidence that life exists or once existed anywhere else in Solar System.

Conclusion

In summary, it is generally accepted by most scientists that life must have originated by chemical evolution, but we cannot be completely sure whether this took place on Earth or whether life originated extraterrestrially. However, on the balance of evidence presented in Book 8, the former alternative is most likely to be correct.

References

De Duve, C. (2003) 'A research proposal on the origin of life', Closing lecture given at the ISSOL Congress, Oaxaca, Mexico on 4 July 2002, *Origin of Life and Evolution of the Biosphere*, 33, 559–574. [Article 2]

Hazan, R. (2005) *Genesis, the Scientific Quest for Life's Origin*, Joseph Henry, Washington DC. [Article 4]

Zahnle, K.J. (2006) 'Earth's earliest atmosphere' *Elements*, 2, 217–222. [Article 3]

Don't be worried if you found this activity difficult; extracting relevant information for an account like this, and particularly deciding which points to include and which to omit really is difficult. So when you compare your plan with the one above, you shouldn't be concerned if some of the points are different. The account you have planned would summarise a lot of information from Sections 2.4.1–2.4.3, and from Articles 2–4, so there is plenty of scope for different approaches. The most important aspects that you should have included are the two possible ways that life might have originated – chemical evolution on Earth and immigration from elsewhere – with some explanation of each of them, together with a comparison of the two ways.

When writing an account in which the information comes mainly from OU texts, or from articles provided by the OU, you should not quote verbatim large sections. Make the points in your own words and then, in brackets, indicate where you got the information, e.g. (Section 2.4.1). Similarly, if you obtained information from non-OU textbooks or websites, then give a reference to these sources. (Recall Section 1.5, where referencing of source materials is discussed.)

Activity 3.1

Task 1

Our summary is given below. You should compare it with yours, and if there is a large difference, compare ours with the article.

In the observed electromagnetic radiation at near-infrared wavelengths there was a strong dip in brightness at 0.76 μm. This is a result of absorption by molecular oxygen, implying that this molecule is abundant in the Earth's atmosphere. Photosynthesis is the only known process that could sustain such large quantities of oxygen.

There was a sharp absorption of radiation with wavelengths of about 0.7 μm, which could not be attributed to any mineral species. Such a feature is not known from any other planet in the Solar System. This feature is from chlorophyll, a green pigment found in plants that absorbs energy from sunlight, thereby enabling photosynthesis.

Within the infrared spectrum there was also a feature resulting from about 1 ppm of methane. This is in extreme disequilibrium with all the oxygen present – without the constant addition of methane to the atmosphere (from bacterial metabolism) it would simply react with the oxygen to produce water and carbon dioxide.

One of the instruments picked up radio emissions that could not be explained by natural sources (such as lightning). The conclusion would have to be that the orderly signals were the product of a technological civilisation. (*194 words*)

Activity 3.2

Task 1

Titan has a very thick atmosphere of nitrogen plus other gases; telescopes from Earth, and the HST and cameras on the *Voyager 2* during its fly-by could not look through this atmosphere to the surface.

Task 2

The features could have been produced either by a liquid or a solid. However, the meandering nature of the features implies they were produced by rivers, rather than glaciers. But the temperature of Titan's surface is close to −200 °C, well below the freezing point of water, so the rivers could not have been of water. They were more likely to be of liquid methane or liquid ethane.

Task 3

Titan's nitrogen atmosphere is also rich in simple organic molecules (methane, ethane) which rain down on to the surface. On Earth, these molecules are thought to have been significant for the chemical reactions that led to the origin of life. And so Titan is regarded as an example of a location where prebiotic chemistry is taking place.

Activity 3.3

Task 1

The five lines of evidence are given in the last paragraph (Extract 2) of Article 6. They relate to the meteorite ALH84001, an igneous Martian rock.

- The rock was penetrated by a fluid along fractures and pore spaces, which then became sites of secondary mineral formation and possible biogenic activity.
- The carbonate globules at these sites have a formation age younger than that of the igneous rock.
- Images of the globules and of other features show a resemblance to terrestrial microorganisms, terrestrial biogenic carbonate structures, or microfossils.
- There are magnetite and iron sulfide particles that could have resulted from oxidation and reduction reactions known to be important in terrestrial microbial systems.
- At surfaces rich in carbonate globules there are polycyclic aromatic hydrocarbons.

Activity 3.4

Task 1

All but one of the Martian meteorites have young crystallisation ages, and this rules out all parent bodies except Venus, the Moon, Earth, Mars, and some of the satellites of the giant planets. Venus is ruled out because rock fragments blasted from its surface would vaporise in the thick atmosphere. The satellites of the giant planets are ruled out because the fragments could not escape their gravitational fields. The Earth and the Moon are ruled out because of the chemistry of the rocks. The Martian meteorites are recognised as a group through their similar oxygen isotopic compositions, different from that of the Earth and the Moon. One of the group contains pockets of gases that have a similar composition to the atmosphere of Mars. (*124 words*)

Task 2

Three sets of information that we can get about Mars from Martian meteorites are: (i) from the main silicate minerals, we can learn about primary igneous processes, i.e. the composition of the magma from which the rocks crystallised; (ii) from secondary phases (carbonates and clay minerals) we can learn about the fluid that altered the rocks after they had crystallised and (iii) from gas trapped in glass produced by shock, we learn about Mars' atmosphere. (*75 words*)

Activity 4.1

(a) A plot of the data is shown in Figure 4.20.

(b) The plot shows that there might be a planet orbiting this star because the radial speed seems to be varying periodically. [The data are slightly irregular because the measurements have a degree of uncertainty.]

(c) The orbital period is about 50 days, with an uncertainty of about ±1 day. [Values up to ±2.5 days – the interval corresponding to the grid spacing – are acceptable.]

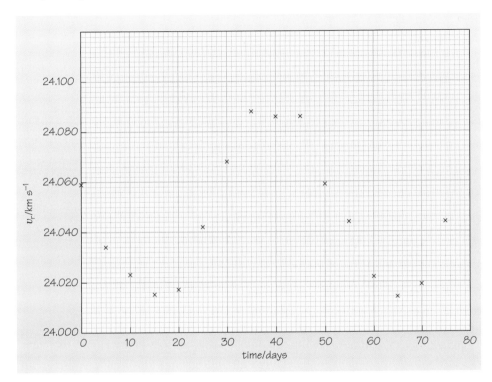

Figure 4.20 The variation in radial speed (magnitude of velocity) of a certain star.

Activity 4.2

Task 1

The detection limits for space-based techniques are always lower than for ground-based techniques because the telescopes are above the atmosphere; the atmosphere decreases and 'blurs' the signal.

Task 2

(a) The planet furthest away from its star is the one with the largest orbital radius and longest orbital period (horizontal axis) – think of how the orbits of Mercury and Neptune differ within the Solar System. Gravitational microlensing techniques (both ground- and space-based) will be able to detect planets further away from their stars than the other methods.

(b) This is because all the other techniques have to observe the star–planet system for a substantial fraction of the orbital period. Planets far away from their stars have orbital periods longer than 10 years, so observation campaigns would have to last for many years in order to detect the such planets. Gravitational microlensing does not need to observe star–planet systems for so long.

(c) The smallest planet is the one with the lowest mass (plotted on the vertical axis). The space-based mission *Kepler* is predicted to detect planets with masses as low as 0.3 Earth mass (slightly smaller than Mercury) as they occult their stars, as long as the planets are less than about 0.01 AU away from their stars (Mercury is about 0.4 AU from the Sun).

Activity 4.3

Task 1

The terms in the Drake equation that can either be measured directly by astronomical techniques, or are potentially predictable on the basis of sound physical models, are R, rate of formation of stars; f_g, fraction of stars suitable for supporting life; f_p, fraction of those stars with planetary systems; n_e, number of planets per planetary system with an environment suitable for life. The remaining terms are much more difficult to predict.

Task 2

Substituting the values into Equation 4.7 gives

$$N = 10 \times 0.5 \times 0.5 \times 2 \times 0.5 \times 0.5 \times 0.5 \times 10\,000$$
$$= 6000 \text{ (to one significant figure)}$$

It is clear that the value of N depends strongly on the values assumed for the terms in the equation. Various authors have reached values of N, anywhere between essentially zero and many millions.

Activity 5.1

The following is an example of an account that attempts to answer the question posed. It uses references to articles when required, also it also gives (in parentheses) appropriate sections of this book so you can see where the information came from and how it was built up from the plan given in the comments to Activity 2.6. While most of the information for this account came directly from this book, some key points were used from three of the articles. Identifying the most appropriate sources of information from a large choice of literature is a key 'information literacy' skill.

From a scientific viewpoint, there are only two ways in which life might have originated on Earth: by the chemical evolution of life from simple chemicals, or by immigration of some form of life from an extraterrestrial source. Both of these mechanisms are described and compared in this account.

A process for the chemical evolution of life is one in which simple molecules such as water, methane, carbon monoxide and ammonia react together to form simple organic molecules such as amino acids and sugars. These then evolve into more complex molecules such as proteins, complex carbohydrates and nucleic acids, from which (eventually) living cells are organised (Section 2.4).

Hypotheses for this process are based either on simulation experiments, for example those by Miller and others (e.g. De Duve, 2003; Hazan, 2005) or on modelling (Zahnle, 2006).

Simple organic molecules might have originated in shallow pools or at ocean surfaces, or on pyrite particles in the atmosphere (Section 2.4.1). A suggestion that they were generated in a strongly reducing atmosphere by the action of UV radiation is now regarded as unlikely. It is also possible that simple organic molecules reached Earth from space via dust particles, comets or meteorites.

The reaction of simple organic molecules to produce more complex organic molecules presumably occurred wherever the feedstock of simple organic molecules was present. Problems that had to be overcome to allow reactions to proceed were those of hydrolysis and also the need to maintain high concentrations of reactants (Section 2.4.1). This led to the suggestion that solid surfaces were important (Hazan, 2005).

The final stage in the chemical evolution of life is the conversion of non-living macromolecules to living cells. It is likely that the first cells were autotrophic (Section 2.4.2). Two important developments must have occurred: the formation of a surrounding membrane and a way to store and replicate information.

Claims for an extraterrestrial origin argue that life, in some heat-resistant form (e.g. spores or single cells protected by layer of carbon – Section 2.5.3) reached Earth on dust particles or via the interior of meteorites. This argument implicitly assumes that life arose by chemical evolution on another planet (or even on comets or asteroids).

One argument initially presented against chemical evolution on Earth was that there was insufficient time between the Earth cooling down and the earliest known life arising (Section 2.5). This argument assumed that the most ancient life on Earth was about 3850 million years old. However, it is currently believed that the oldest life on Earth is about 3400 million years old (Section 2.2), leaving an ample 1200 million years for life to evolve. A further argument against an extraterrestrial origin is that it is thought unlikely that organisms could survive for long periods in space, or survive the rapid descent through Earth's atmosphere (Section 2.5).

In summary, it is generally accepted by most scientists that life must have originated by chemical evolution, but we cannot be completely sure whether this took place on Earth or whether life originated extraterrestrially. However, on the balance of evidence presented in Book 8, the former alternative is most likely to be correct. (*521 words*)

References

Burchell, M.J. (2006) 'W(h)ither the Drake equation?', *International Journal of Astrobiology*, 5(5), 243–250. [Article 9]

De Duve, C. (2003) 'A research proposal on the origin of life', Closing lecture given at the ISSOL Congress, Oaxaca, Mexico on 4 July 2002, *Origins of Life and Evolution of the Biosphere*, 33, 559–574. [Article 2]

Dominik, M., Horne, K. and Bode, M. (2006) 'The first cool rocky/icy exoplanet', *Astronomy and Geophysics*, 47, 3.25–3.30.

Encyclopedia of Astronomy and Astrophysics, (2001) [online] Macmillan. [Article 8]

Hazan, R. (2005) *Genesis, the Scientific Quest for Life's Origin*, Joseph Henry, Washington DC. [Article 4]

Lebreton, J.-P. (2006) 'Tuning in to Titan', *Physics World*, 19(2), 20–23. [Article 6]

Lepland, A., van Zuilen, M.A., Arrhenius, G., Whitehouse, M.J. and Fedo, C.M. (2005) 'Questioning the evidence for Earth's earliest life – Akilia revisited', *Geology*, 33, 77–79.

McKay, D.S., Gibson Jr., E.K., Thomas-Keprta, K.L., Vali, H., Romanek, C.S., Clemett, S.J., Chillier, X.D.F., Maechling, C.R. and Zare, R.N. (1996) 'Search for past life on Mars: possible relic biogenic activity in Martian meteorite ALH84001', *Science*, 273, 924–930. [Article 7]

Mojzsis, S.J., Arrhenius, G., McKeegan, K.D., Harrison, T.M., Nutman, A.P. and Friend, C.R.L. (1996) 'Evidence for life on Earth before 3,800 million years ago', *Nature*, 384, 55–59.

Moorbath, S. (2005) 'Dating eariest life', *Nature*, 434, 155. [Article 1]

Sagan, C. (1994) 'The search for extraterrestrial life', *Scientific American*, 271(4), 70–77. [Article 5]

Schidlowski, M. (1988) 'A 3,800-million-year isotopic record of life from carbon in sedimentary rocks', *Nature*, 333, 313–318.

Zahnle, K.J. (2006) 'Earth's earliest atmosphere', *Elements*, 2, 217–222. [Article 3]

Acknowledgements

The S104 course team gratefully acknowledges the contributions of the S103 *Discovering science* course team and of its predecessors.

Grateful acknowledgement is made to the following sources for permission to reproduce material in this book:

Text

Article 1: Moorbath, S. (2005) 'Dating earliest life', Nature, vol. 434, 10 March 2005, © *Nature* Publishing;

Figures

Cover: Eric Heller/Science Photo Library;

Figure 2.2: Schidlowski, M. (1988) 'A 3800 million year isotopic record of life', *Nature*, vol. 333, 26 May 1988 copyright 1988 © Macmillan Magazines Ltd.; Figure 2.3: Commonwealth Palaeontological Collections of the Australian Geological Society; Figure 2.4: Courtesy of Professor Andrew Knoll; Figure 2.5: Gray, M.W. (1996) 'A Third form of life', *Nature*, vol. 383, 26 September 1996, © Macmillan Magazines Ltd.; Figures 2.8a and 2.8b: © Woods Hole Oceanographic Institution;

Figure 3.2: NASA/Johns Hopkins University Applied Laboratory/Carnegie Institution of Washington; Figure 3.3: ESA/MPAE, 1986, 1996; Figure 3.4a, 3.6a, 3.b, 3.6c, 3.7, 3.11, 3.13 and 3.14: NASA/JPL-Caltech; Figure 3.4b: NASA/JSC; Figure 3.5: Hubble Space Telescope Comet Team and NASA; Figure 3.8: © European Space Agency; Figure 3.9: NASA/JPL/Space Science Institute; Figure 3.10: © European Space Agency; Figure 3.12a: NASA/JPL-Caltech/USGS/Cornell; Figure 3.12b: NASA/JPL/Cornell;

Figure 4.1: David A. Hardy, Futures: 50 years in space/Science Photo Library; Figure 4.12: Al Schultz (CSC/STScI and NASA); Figure 4.13: C.R. O'Dell/Rice University; NASA; Figure 4.18: ESO.

Every effort has been made to contact copyright holders. If any have been inadvertently overlooked the publishers will be pleased to make the necessary arrangements at the first opportunity.

The S104 course team

Chair

Valda Stevens

Deputy Chair and Academic Editor

Neil McBride

Course Manager

Arabelle Sexton

Authors

John Baxter
Stuart Bennett
Stephen Blake
Diane Butler
Steve Drury
Mike Gillman
Monica Grady
Ellen Heeley

Sally Jordan
Neil McBride
Judith Metcalfe
Andrew Norton
Stephen Serjeant
Sandy Smith
David Robinson

External Course Assessor

Dr Andy Platt (University of Staffordshire)

Production Team

Steve Best (*Media Developer*)
Greg Black (*Media Developer*)
Joe Buchanan (*Media Developer*)
Martin Chiverton (*Producer*)
Roger Courthold (*Media Developer*)
James Davies (*Media Project Manager*)
Lydia Eaton (*Media Assistant*)
Emily Fuller (*Media Assistant*)
Rebecca Graham (*Media Developer*)
Michael Francis (*Media Developer*)
Sara Hack (*Media Developer*)
Rafael Hidalgo (*Media Project Manager*)
Sarah Hofton (*Media Developer*)

Chris Hough (*Media Developer*)
Gareth Hudson (*Media Developer*)
Jason Jarratt (*Media Developer*)
Martin Keeling (*Media Assistant*)
Corinne Owen (*Media Assistant*)
Lucy Owens (*S&V Co-ordinator*)
Deana Plummer (*Media Assistant*)
Will Rawes (*Media Developer*)
Andy Sutton (*Media Developer*)
Fiona Thomson (*Media Developer*)
Pamela Wardell (*Media Developer*)
Clare Withers (*Course Team Assistant*)

Other contributors

Amongst the many people who helped in various ways in the production of S104 the Course Team would like to thank the following people for their contributions:

Tom Argles (*Earth Sciences multimedia*)

Patricia Ash (*Study Skills*)

Chris Ashley (*Critical Reader*)

Yvonne Ashmore (*Books 4 and 5 Chemdraw*)

Kate Bradshaw (*Book 6 multimedia*)

Mark Brandon (*Critical Reader*)

Charles Cockell (*Critical Reader*)

Eleanor Crabb (*Book 4 multimedia*)

Janet Haresnape (*Book 5 multimedia*)

Richard Jordan (*Multimedia and iCMA checker*)

Stephen Larkin (*Critical Reader*)

Jennifer Matthews (*Critical Reader*)

Ian Parkinson (*Earth sciences assessment*)

Shelagh Ross (*Book 3 video*)

Claire Rothwell (*Tutor resources*)

Jonathan Silvertown (*Book 5 multimedia*)

Kiki Warr (*Critical Reader*)

Peter Webb (*Critical Reader*)

Index

Entries and page numbers in **bold type** refer to key words that are printed in **bold** in the text and that are defined in the glossary. Where the page number is given in *italics*, the index information is carried mainly or wholly in an illustration or table.